Event Management

A Booming Industry and an Eventful Career

Event Management

A Booming Industry and an Eventful Career

Devesh Kishore
Ganga Sagar Singh

HAR-ANAND
PUBLICATIONS PVT LTD

Reprint, 2026

Published by Ashok Gosain and Ashish Gosain for
HAR-ANAND PUBLICATIONS PVT LTD
E-49/3, Okhla Industrial Area, Phase-II, New Delhi-110020
Tel: 41603491
E-mail: info@haranandbooks.com/haranand@rediffmail.com
Shop online at: www.haranandbooks.com

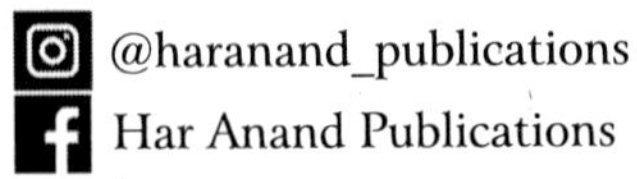

Printed in India at Megha Enterprises

PREFACE

The event planning and management industry has an extremely positive future. In addition to the usual corporate meetings, trade shows, and conferences, the event planning industry has also gotten involve in the advertising and branding efforts of their clients. Event planners, who can identify their clients' branding strategies and can bring their expertise of running the logistic of live event, have a very popular future. According to Larry Jaeger, President, Events Xtraordinaire, "Any marketing majors who are looking for a growing and lucrative niche should definitely consider a career in event branding and experiential marketing."

Event Industry is yet in premature stage in India and it has lots of potential in it and job market is still to be explored fully. But, of late, event management has emerged as the fastest growing industry in India. Simultaneously, event management has turned out to be blossoming and meaningful career for professionals.

According to a study conducted by FICCI, event management is a multi-crore industry with mega shows and events regularly hosted in India. Event expenses which were 20 crore during 1990, grew to 500 crore by 2000. According to an estimate of the FICCI, event management industry is going to be a 3,500 crore industry by 2005 and is likely to be 10,000, crore by the end of 2011.

As conglomerate of a number of professions, the event management as a profession is still and continues to be a complex learning situation for young students. It is basically an extension of public relations and corporate communication. It has branched off from public relations. After all, the event management includes a number of qualities and skills of technological knowledge, organizational skills, public relations, marketing, advertising, catering, logistics, décor, human relations, risk management and above all in media handling and working of various media.

But due to the shortage of trained event managers, companies are not finding their executives fully equal to the task to manage the events, specially when required of international standards. By now, a number of institutes, both in government and private sectors, have started imparting training and formal education in Event Management. But still they lack facilities and infrastructure of international standards to trend the event managers.

Due to shortage of Faculty for formal education in Event Management discipline, the demand for trained event management personnel, is far exceeding the supply. To fill in the existing gap between the demand and supply, some big business houses have now initiated training their executives in event management.

In view of the above mentioned factors and requirements of event industry it has been the efforts to present a book on Event Management which may prove to the extent possible, as a guide to all the stakeholders. These stakeholders may be future entrepreneurs in the field of event industry, persons in the field of event management profession and learners of event management i.e. students.

To understand any concept or a profession, it is necessary to define it. Chapter I deals with the definition the types and advantages of event management. This has been followed by creative visualization and design of event management. Event sponsorship is a *sine quanon* for organizing any event management. The success of any event management and its viability depend largely on its marketing and promotion. This is followed by planning techniques and procedures to organize an event which is the first step in any event management. While staging an event, it is necessary to ensure and take all precautionary measures for safety and security for both the staff and audience, with crowd management and evacuation plans in place. Monitoring, control and evaluation are necessary for any industry or profession to flourish. Evaluation helps to find out the shortcomings in staging any event and make necessary improvements in organizing any such event in future.

Like any other profession, Event Management has also its own code of ethics. The observance of the ethics of any profession helps in maintaining and improving the image of the profession high in comparison to other similar profession

All these points and factors have been mentioned in the book in separate chapters, specially for easy comprehension of the students of event management.

Hope this book will prove as a philosopher of industry, guide to practicing professionals and a friend of future event manager.

DR. DEVESH KISHORE
GANGA SAGAR SINGH

CONTENTS

1

INTRODUCTION

Definition

Professor Donand Getz (1997), a well-known writer in the field of event management, defines special events from two perspectives, that of customer and that of event manager, as follows:

- A special event is a one-time or infrequently occurring event outside normal programme or activity of the sponsoring or organizing body.
- To the customer or guest a special event is an opportunity for leisure, social or cultural experience outside the normal range of choices or beyond everyday experience.

Dr J Goldblatt (1997) defines special events as "A unique moment in the time celebrated with ceremony and ritual to satisfy specific needs."

The wide range of events may include special events such as, sporting events, corporate meetings, conventions, expositions, festivals, carnivals, prize-distribution ceremonies, etc

Size of Events

In terms of size, events may be categorized as

(a) Mega Events,

(b) Regional Events, and

(c) Major Events and Minor Events.

Mega Events: The largest event are called mega-events which are generally targeted at international level. The Olympic Games, World Cup Soccer, Commonwealth Games, may be good examples of mega events. It is televised to a large scale across the world and adds millions to local economy. All such events have a specific yield in terms of tourism, media coverage and revenue earning and resultant economy impact. A number of cities and governments are vying with one another to host such mega events.

Although the Olympic Games, the Commonwealth Games, etc may be put in the category of mega events due to its size in terms of expenditure, sponsorship, economic impact and audience round- the-globe, it is worth comparing some other events in terms of its size. For example, Maha Kumbh Mela, 2001, was the largest religious gathering in the history of man kind. During the Mela (event) approximately 70 million Hindu pilgrims converged on the confluence of Ganga Yamuna and Saraswati rivers at Sangam in Allahabad (UP), India, for a sacred bathing ritual, that devotees believe, will purify all the sins of persons taking a holy dip there. The event takes place every 12 years. The 2001 congregation, described as the "Greatest Show on Earth" was the largest gathering of humanity ever in any single event of the world.

Regional Events

Regional events are designed to increase the appeal of a specific tourism destination or region. Some examples are, FAN Fare, the biggest country music festival of the world held annually in Nashville, etc, of tourist destination both for domestic and international tourism markets through their annual events.

Major Events

Major events attract significant local interest and participants in large numbers and also generate tourism revenue in huge quantity. For example, Chinese New Year celebrations are held in many capital cities. Friends and relatives of the Chinese community invariably visit during the celebrations. Most major cities have a convention center capable of holding large meetings, trade shows and convention. The India International Trade Fair Authority has a permanent venue namely, Pragati Maidan in Delhi to organize international trade fair annually on fixed dates (19-25 November). Similarly Vigyan Bhawan in New Delhi is a big convention hall to hold international meeting.

Minor Events: Almost every town, city and state in India host annual events. Most events fall into this category, and it is here that most event managers gain their experience. In the category of agricultural fairs and expos, there are literally thousands of national, state and regional events which are held each year in India. In addition, there are many one-time events including historical, cultural, musical and dance performances. For example, India International Film Festival is organized every year. Now, there is a fixed centre in Goa as a permanent venue for International Film Festival Meetings, parties, celebrations, conventions, award ceremonies, exhibitions sporting events come into the category of Minor Events.

Types of Events

In terms of type, events may be categorized as: **Sporting Events, Entertainment, Art and Culture Events, Festival Events and Family Events.**

Sporting Events: Sporting events are held in all towns, cities, state capitals, through out the country. They attract international sports men and women at different levels they include football, cricket, wrestling, athletics, hockey, car racing. These major events are matched at the local levels by sporting competitions at all levels. For example, Interstate police athletic meet, inter-university athletic meet etc are organized. Firstly, competitions are organized at district and college levels and then inter-district and inter-college tournaments are organized which culminates into inter-state police meet and inter-university competitive events.

Entertainment, Arts and Culture Events

Entertainment events attract large number of audience. In some cases, the concerts are quite viable from financial point of view. However, in some cases, financial problems can quickly escalate when sales of tickets do not reach targets. In some cases, entertainment events had to be canceled on account of payment/no payment to artists, poor arrangement at the sight of event or objections by the district administration on the ground of law and order problems.

Commercial Marketing and Promotional Events

Promotional events involve product launches. The aim of product launches/ promotional events is to generally differentiate the products from its competitors and ensure that it is distinguished and memorable. The audience of a promotional activity might be sales staff such as travel agent who would promote the tour to their clients or potential purchasers, the media are usually invited to these events, so that both impact and risk are high.

Festivals

Food festivals are increasingly providing an opportunity to showcase its products. In USA many wine regions hold festival, often in combination with musical events, such as Portland Jazz Festival. Religious festivals also fall into this category. Durga Puja and Diwali are examples of religious festivals in India. Festivals on the eve of harvesting of crops in India are also good examples and fall into the categories. Bihu of Assam, Onam of Kerala and Baisakhi of Punjab are good example of festival events, celebrated annually on a large scale with enthusiasm and religious fervor. Chinese New Year, and Championship Native American POW Wow at Traders Village, Texas, are good examples.

Family Events

Weddings, anniversaries and now funerals also provide opportunities for families to get together. It adds more crowds and colors if it is the wedding is of a celebrity, whether be from sports, film or political personality. It is both pain and pleasure that accompany a funeral procession. In case of the premature death of a person, pain and grief are the natural phenomenon, on the other hand it is a celebration all over with some faint sense of loss, to bid farewell to a grand old man/ women, on his or her demise. It is important for an event manager to keep a track of these changing social trends.

It has been observed that most common events are community related and they are run on fairly small scale with voluntary support and sponsorship. These events provide the potential event managers with wide range of experience and opportunity to contribute to their community. Every event has some purpose and a theme is generally linked to the purpose. But there are certain principles that apply to managing all events.

Advantages of Events

Events play an important role in promoting an organization, particularly a specific brand. Under stiff competitions, organizations plan events to interact with partners of the trade along with potential customers. Events are targeted towards specific segments of the market. Their remains a option of selective audience and selective exposure. It is the responsibility of event experts to invite only target audience which would benefit from the event depending on the venue where the event is being organized and the brain being offered through the event. Whenever an individual attends an event, he expects to get benefitted from the event. Visitors are the target and asset of the event, because a satisfy visitor works as a volunteer and opinion leader in time to come.

Events are an open forum where the participants meet the actual users as well as the middleman of the trade. Direct contact with all segments of the target audience, provides immediate feedback related to the success and failure of the event and help the organizers to develop future marketing plans on the basis of feedback received at the time of event. This explains the need for the event and its successful planning. Event management is now a necessity and part of corporate policy planning. The motive behind organizing events may be different in corporate and non- profit organizations, the importance of event planning remains the same in all working environment.

"Act local, think globally" has become the mantra of the last century. Events organization is now interrelated to Corporate Social Responsibility (CSR) and Corporate Citizenship philosophy. According to CB Bhattacharya, E ON Chair Professor of European School of Management and Technology (ESMT) Berlin, 'Corporate Social Responsibility is today an integral part of a majority of companies' marketing strategy world wide'. He further adds that it is the "biggest movement not because it is fashionable but a license to operate in a competitive market characterized by increasing stakeholder consciousness." The key global challenges for responsible business, it is the combine of 'doing well' and with 'doing good', he adds "if a company can prove its sincerity and motives behind their CSR efforts, this reservoir of goodwill will pay off," he says

On an effective CSR initiative in India he cited the example of Hindustan Unilever's 'Washing Hands' campaign. "It was an effective campaign in rural areas (which was the target segment) and had both social and business outcomes," Bhattacharya said.

Events organized by Grasim Industries are interrelated with the concept of corporate citizenship philosophy of the organization. The stress on corporate citizenship has turned the decision-making capacity of the corporate organizations into a serious act at all levels of the management. Creativity plays an important role as it sells both good and services, though finance plays the vital role. But the role of creativity and the work of creative professionals can not be disregarded in any form.

Knowledge industries are going to transfer itself into a trade opportunity in coming years. Full circle publishing houses have well planned policy to interact with its target audience the publishing houses plan event to come closer to its target audience who come to visit and enjoy the events. These events give the audience an opportunity to interact with customer and sales take places at these events indirectly. Business development depends on the capability of the organizers to plan event, exhibitions and trade fares. An expert event manager can be successful with minimum possibility of error, if he plans events properly.

Event Management for Non-Profit Organization

Events are important and they turned out to be more helpful for non-profit organizations. As business organizations plan proposals to tackle a target audience, for the same an NGO opts for the segments which it wants to serve. But it is difficult for any NGO, when it intends to cover the entire population with special needs of a country like India. Lack of sufficient resources is the greatest handicap for an NGO in any such situation. It is expected that the pressure on NGOs will increase, with the increase in the number of people with special needs during coming years.

Decision Making

Decision making is both a managerial and organizational process. In organizational process many decisions transcend the individual planner and become the product of group or team decisions. In the managerial decision, the decision making is the responsibility of a manager in giving a shape to the planning of an organization or choosing alternatives. Managers need to develop necessary skill of decision making and problem solving to take decisions. Decision making skills hold a central place and is an inherent or in-built functions in all managerial responsibilities. For example, in planning one has to take decision for setting objectives, scheduling the concept, budgeting, etc similarly in organizations, decisions have to be taken regarding delegating the authority of project implementations, establishment of communication channels and the likes.

Decision making involves three aspects of human behavior; **Cognition, Conation and Affection.** Cognition is an activity of mind associated with knowledge. Conation is the action of mind implied by words such as willingness, desire and aversion. Affection is an aspect of mind associated with emotion, feeling, mood and temperament. Generally decision making and planning are taken as the same. But for management experts these are two are different. One can take decision for many activities but the decision will be implemented only through planning. Also the role of decision making is highly important in planning. Managers follow certain steps which help them to understand the decision making process and to provide a process to be adopted for a rational decision making. Decision making is like conducting a research to find answers to hidden problems, which are necessary for an organization or a manager to solve them for further development in his stream.

Events differ in different cultural and economic condition of the people around the event venue. Event planners adopt strategic planning for rapping their events in the subtle layers of planning elements designed to evoke hidden desires of the spectators. The purpose of holding an event is to achieve the objectives of the organizer. These objectives can be both internal and external. The internal objectives of the organizer are company mandated. Event planning is the most important ingredient in the process of event management. The proposal meeting is for the event planner to understand the objectives of the company. External objectives are the hidden agenda of the client who wants the event planner to complete even without disclosing the secret wishes.

EVENT INDUSTRIES IN INDIA

Present Situation

Image management and event industries in India, both are attracting

More and more sections of the society at large. Corporate organization and non-profit organizations, both want good media coverage in print as well as electronic media. To achieve this, all had appointed experts in the fields of Public Relations, Corporate Communication and Event Management. Event planning plays an important role for propagating organization's point of view. Now-a-days, it can be observed that the organization is not in news in spite of organizing a series of events, seminars and conferences. It may be an indication of a weak image management and poor brand positioning.

CODE OF ETHICS

A code of ethics for event industries can enhance the reputations of those involved and assist customers to feel confident in their choice of event manager.

International Special Events Society (ISPS) has devised the following code of ethics:

- Promote and increase the highest level of ethics within the profession of the special event industries, while maintaining the highest standard of professional conduct,
- Strive for excellence in all aspects of our profession by performing consistently at par or above excepted industries standards,
- Use only legal and ethical means in all industries negotiations and activities,
- Protect the public against fraud and unfair practices and promote all practices which bring credit to the profession,
- Maintain adequate and appropriate insurance coverage for all business activities,
- Maintain industry standard of safety and sanitation,
- Provide truthful and accurate information with respect to the performance of duties. Use a written contract stating all changes, services, products, performance expectations and other essential information,

- Commit to increase professional growth and knowledge, to attain educational programmes and to personally contribute expertise to meetings and journals,
- Strive to cooperate with colleagues and suppliers, employees/ employers and all persons supervise, in order to provide the highest quality of service at every level,
- Subscribe to the ISES Principles of Professional Conduct and Ethics, and abide by ISES Bye-laws and Policy.

SUGGESTED QUESTIONS

1. Define Event Management.
2. What is the importance of customer in event management?
3. What is the role of event manager in special event?
4. What is the importance of event in the promotion of an organization?
5. What is Corporate Social Responsibility? How Indian Corporate is sincere in performing their responsibility?
6. What is the status of event industries in India?
7. How a code of ethics can enhance the reputation of the professionals involved in event management?
8. What is the Code of Ethics divide by ISES?

2

Creative Visualization and Design of Event Management

Success of any event depends on the use of creativity in the event. Creativity is being encouraged both in large institutions, service industries and the product selling industries. Every individual has some kind of creative patch inside him. But many of us are not able to explore our own strengths. That hinders a person to deliver as per the expectations of the social culture.

Creative Visualizations

Creativity and managerial skills are the inherent traits required in any one looking for a carrier in event management. Event planners are essentially required to be cool, composed creative, communicative and calculative. Creativity has a lot to do and creative individuals are always assumed to be the most successful professionals in the field of Event Management. Event industry is one of the highly paying industries and the experts who work in the field are quite enthusiastic and confident in their profession.

Stevan Harnad University of Southampton Highfield defines creativity as follows: The concept of creativity is very difficult to define and understand. At times a person think of himself as a creative individual and some time later he gets frustrated when he fails in visualizing a particular idea in an acceptable fashion. Creative individuals tend to manifest certain characteristics that they are ready to inter into risk, they have a sense of humor and are persons of divergent thinking. The consultant and researchers are of the view that the easiest way for people to be creative is to think out-of-the box, to break their paradigms or mind sets and have their own ways of thinking. The success of every event depends to a large extent upon the way they encourage the use of creativity in their events.

According to Pasteurs: "…. le hazard favorise l'esprit prepare (chance favors the prepared mind)" Pasteur was speaking about a very specific kind of creativity, namely, experimental scientific creativity. Pasteur's in sight seems to apply as aptly to all forms of creativity. There is an element of chance in creativity but it is most likely to occur if the mind is prepared for it. Pasteur did not mean being born with "creative" trait rather he meant that existing knowledge and skills relevant to the creative leap had to be sufficiently master before a fall of something from no where. His suggestion for creativity is the most uncreative one imaginable, which is to learn what is already known. Creativity has to do something with originality and novelty. However it can not just be equivalent to something new and not only new. Something creative must also have some value relative to what already exists and what is perceived as being needed. However there are many cognitive activities that are ordinarily not creative in themselves, each one of them is capable of being performed creatively as well. So a creativity is some how complementary to ordinary cognition.

Creativity: A Method or a Magic ?

Generation gap, most of the times, creates problems as youngsters don't want to be reached. Event planning can turn out to be hell lot of work, which could be very stressful, but when experts undertake planning then results might surprise a lot of people. As artists, we often have a few moments to make impression. To keep the viewer interested, to make them want to take a closer look. It can be hard sometimes, as becoming attached, means letting go, if it is your living.

Remember, if some one else feels the same they may want to own it. If your work make people nostalgic, happy, excited or start a conversation with you it can be incredibly fulfilling. What is "Creativity"? Is it a cognitive trait that some people have and others do not have? Is it an occasional state that people sometimes enter into it? Or is it defined completely by its products: "Creativity is as creativity does"? Whatever it is, how does creativity come about? How do you do it? What are their results? Will practice help make you to be a creative?

There is probably some truth in all three notions of what creativity is. It is a trait, because it is statistical facts that some individuals exhibit it repeatedly. It may also be correlated with some other traits. Some even think, it can be predicted by objective psychological tests. But it is also obviously a state, because no one is creative all the time and some people are highly creative only once in their lives. There are a number of concepts in the air about the underlined mechanisms of creativity, theories attributing it to everything from method to madness-none of them very satisfactory. As to inducing creativities-by using heuristic strategies or through "Creativity training"—this has had very limited success.

CONCEPTS OF CREATIVITY METHODS

The famous dictum of Pasteur, ... le hassard favorise l'esprit prepare ("chance favors the prepared mind"), will turn out to say more what can be said about creativity than the more ambitious or modern notions. Pasteur was speaking, of course, about a very specific kind of creativities. (The quote actually begins: "In the experimental fields" or "In the fields of experimentation," and was in part concerned with the question of whether the experimental discovery, the so called "serendipitous" once—are really just lucky accidents). Pasteur's insight applies just as apply to all forms of creativity, however.

Creativity is most likely to occur if the mind is some what prepared for it, but there is an element of chance also in creativity. Context shows that by "preparation", Pasteur did not mean by being born with "creative" trait. He meant that existing knowledge and skills relevant to the creative "leap" first had to be sufficiently mastered before a likely "bolt from the blue." Paradoxically, his suggestion is that the only formula for the creativity is the most uncreative one imaginable, which is to learn what is already known. Only then you are likely to have enough of the requisite raw materials for an original contribution and only then would you even be in a position to recognize something worthwhile and original for what it was.

There are four theories about the underlying mechanism of creativity. They can be classified as:

(I) Method,

(II) Memory,

(III) Magic, and

(IV) Mutation.

The Method view is that there is a formula for creativity. The Memory view is that the essential factor is somehow innate. The Magic view is that mysterious, unconscious, inexplicable forces are involved. And the Mutation view is that the essential element is chance.

Creativity as the working of the unconscious mind is the class of Magic theories. The problem of explaining creative and non-creative cognition consists of providing a mechanism for all our unconscious processing. The only formatting aspects of the unconscious mind model is the attention it draws to the completeness of the role of conscious deliberate efforts, in the creative process.

A Memory theory holds that creativity is somehow guided by the innate structure of mind. This theory at first seems to apply more to intellectual creativity than to artistic creativity. The view seems to attribute too much to inner structure of mind without giving any explanation of its nature and origins.

The Magic theory offers no real explanation of the creative process, merely attributing to mysterious unconscious mind and creativity as the working of the unconscious mind.

The Mutation theory is also called Cerebral Serendipity theory, the school to which Einstein and Poi Care belonged. The scenario is one of gathering together the elements and constraints out of which a creative solution is to arise. This view provides an important clarification of the role of preparation, without preparation.

Concept of the Event

The elements considered in development of an event concept include; the purpose of the event; the theme of the event; the venue of the event; the audience of the event; the timing of the event and available resources and skills of the organizing team of the event.

Purpose of the Event

The purpose of the event should drive. There could be two different purposes if one was to organize a conference for financial planners:

(I) To facilitate an exchange of information about the latest changes in financial planning software products. The focus of the purpose is information.

(II) To achieve an out-of-body experience for financial planners in order to develop a positive association with a new software product. The focus of the purpose is entertainment.

Although for many event organizers the main purpose is to make a profit but for many it is not. A number of events are organized with a community purpose also.

Theme of the Event

The theme of the event should be linked to the purpose. Simultaneously, it should be compatible with the needs of the guests and consistent in all respects. Most events adopt a color scheme that is repeated on all items produce for the event, such as tickets, programmes, uniforms, décor, posters and merchandise. The technique helps to identify with the theme.

Venue of the Event

The implications of choosing an unusual venue instead of a standard venue need to be considered carefully. Decoration is required to match the theme. Lighting, sound and catering also put challenge in unusual settings. The overall strategy to be taken into account is selecting an event venue, should be fit the same with client's and audience's needs at the lowest possible cost.

Audience of the Event

While organizing an event, the needs of all participants need to be considered before finalizing the concept. The special needs, if any, of the audience should be considered and provided. Of course, every audience is different and the event manager needs to go with the flow and direct the event to meet the audience response. The method may involve sudden changes in plan.

Timing of the Event

The timing of the event is often linked to weather or season. In deciding the timing of the event the following four time related factors must be taken into account;

(i) Season;
(ii) Day of the week;
(iii) Time of day and
(iv) Duration

Generally, the weather affects an events an event. Depending on the type of event, too much heat or heavy rain fall, could determine the success of an event. Certain times of the year seem to have over packed with festival events. It is also called festival season October-March in India. Wise event planners take into consideration the time of the year, weather patterns and already scheduled events that may draw attendance.

Event Team and other Stakeholders

The skills of the event team are an important consideration in terms of concept of the event development. It is because the staff, who are working at most events, have very limited time and opportunity for training. In addition stakeholders such as the police, emergency services and the environment protection agencies have all sorts of requirement that could challenge the feasibility of an event and these must be looked into carefully and diligently.

While analyzing an event some more elements are required to be taken into consideration at length. These may be competition, law and regulation, marketing, community impact risk, revenue, expenditure, etc.

An analysis of competition involves looking at the timing and duration of other events, even if they are unrelated. Because people have limited time and disposable income and can spare the same for this purpose from their tourist budgets. A wide range of law and regulations have an impact on the staging of events and it requires event manager's liaison with local or state governments. The marketing efforts are crucial for initial planning. The selection of time and medium/channel of advertisement is most important. The key is to know your valuable customer/audience and become also visible to them. All these require the decision-making skill on the part of the event manager or the event management team.

The impact of an event on the local community is a major consideration of planning. It is essential impacts that are considered in the event proposal. Measures to counteract the impact of weather are an integral part of event feasibility planning. Insurance premiums will also be linked to the perceived risk to the safety of all participants. The investment in event design needs a very careful and professional analysis.

Designing the Event

Event designer always keeps the objectives of the client into consideration, before starting the planning process. The event planners work on the guidelines given by the client event designer, need to develop plan of action for the event and look at how they can use the event as a medium to reach them closer to the goal of the client. The event planner might have been given the basic outline that the client would like to take place,

Strategic event planner designs events to achieve the objectives of their client. Each aspect of the event element is considered from the point of view as to how they can contribute to the success of the event. Each event element is targeted to address a specific area and is layered one on top the other, leading the event move forward and to contribute to meeting the event goals.

Event designer would be interested in drafting a plan which would look both attractive and would be easy to work out. While planning an event the event designer might come up with certain ideas which may look outstanding but might seem to be impossible at the time of arranging the concrete plan for the event. To avoid any such situation the event planner may revise the plan, but see to it that the juice of the creativity flows in the right direction and every idea proves feasible and within the budget limit of the client.

Designing an event is a creative process. Consistency and links to the purpose of the event are essential parts of this process. For this the following creative elements are required to be considered:

Theme, Layout, Décor, Suppliers, Technical Requirements, Entertainment, Catering, etc

Theme: As Goldblatt (1997) points out, the theme should ideally appeal to all senses; tactile, taste, visual and auditory. If the aim of the event is to create a unique and memorable experience for the audience than appealing to all senses will contribute positively to the outcome. The needs of the audience are to be kept in mind, when planning an event.

Layout: This creative element is very often given little consideration. The result is, audience is feeling socially uncomfortable, may be due to too much open space or being a cramped space, having too much light or not sufficient light, limited space between two sitting lines or sitting too far away from one another, etc. The audience needs to comfortably fill the venue to create a positive ambience.

Décor: Fabrics, decorative items, drapes and table settings should be selected and put to suit the event theme, after careful consideration and financially economic. Careful placement of plural arrangements should be made on table stands when being use to decorate the table. Plural arrangements provide a pleasant and appealing to aesthetic sense.

Suppliers: A good relation with suppliers will ensure the supply of quality products of all items/commodities. During most large event, suppliers are hard pressed for best quality products, at a time when volumes are much larger than usual. Under such a situation, only a good-long-standing relationship with the suppliers becomes invaluable.

Technical Requirement: The technical glitches are a common feature of an event or a meeting. Technical glitches by suppliers are unforgivable. Microphones should have backups, the power supply must be ensured, stages and video screens visible to all in the audience. New technology used to demonstrate new products, needs to be thoroughly tested, through repeated rehearsals, beforehand. A backup system is a must. There are times, when a particular event concept should remain just that and not to be carried further, as it is technically almost impossible.

Entertainment: The entertainment should suit the purpose of the event and not to detract from it. The needs of the event audience must be considered carefully and diligently before taking the decision. A clown creating balloon art may be considered for children's parties.

Catering: Delays in supply should be avoided and the quality control of food items be ensured. Food quality and selection are also important. Creative event planning frequently requires unique or unusual food and beverage products and these may take time to find. Time is money and both can contribute to an escalation of costs.

Logistics of Concept: Logistical elements of an event concept must include the following:

Access to the site Physical limitations; Dimensions of the site; Refrigerated storage, Physical space for food preparation; Restroom facilities; Cleaning; Safety; provisions of basic services like Water, Toilet, uninterrupted power supply, etc.

Balance between decision making aspects: Finally and conclusively, in brief, an event concept requires a careful balance between the creative and rational aspects of decision-making. Brainstorming by the planning team will generate ideas, but then these need to be considered and included as to their feasibility and to their compatibility to the event concept.

For future event designs, images should be collected from a range of sources, including magazines, gift wraps, table napkins cards and posters. For a successful and efficient event manager it must be conducted as a continuous process, rather a matter of habits of routine nature.

PARTICIPATION PLANNING IN EVENTS

Trade shows is an important medium to project material, products, services and ideas of an organizations to the public at large. The aim is to develop and increase awareness about the brand name of the company and its products to boost sales. Specialized events of the short duration is organized in the trade fares through out the world, as the general trade fair has lost its significance except for consumer goods. The participation in trade shows enables an organization to display its product, before a large audience. The decision to participate can be taken after ensuring that the audience in the trade shows is those that can not be reached effectively through other promotional activities. It is assumed that public relations, publicity, advertising and sales promotion are used to promote the objectives of the organization by promoting a common thing, which can give a favorable result.

While planning for participation in the trade fare, event or exhibitions make sure that which of the product is the right one to be displayed. A decision about a particular product to be shown is to be taken well in advance. Often, trade magazines publish special features in collaboration with the trade shows organizations and the magazines need photographs and other publicity materials. Research plays an important role in planning as well as promoting events. Event planners must always be aware of what special additions are coming up and with what deadline schedules. Promoters should think of the new model that is being displayed. Trade shows exhibition should reveal innovation and newness.

Every event planner and event organizer should give preference to local promotional efforts. Mere participation in a trade fare or exhibition can not provide desired results as expected by the organizers. It is necessary to evaluate whether the whole exercise was performed as planned and its amounts of success in achieving the desire results.

Event planning being the most important task in organizing the event, exhibitions, trade as well as fairs, need thorough research and careful understanding of the need and desire of the client. The client might request something that could be impossible to provide but it is essential for event planner to provide the client something that could benefit the client in the budget approved for the purpose of organizing an event or exhibition. While working as a public relations expert in any corporate organization the expert should thoroughly go through the proposals before short-listing any event planner to give a presentation on the event proposal. Scrutiny of most efficient event planning agency is not the only task which is usually handled by the communication expert but the task of successful organization of the event which is usually handled by the communication experts. In addition it is the responsibility of the public relations professional to suggest the most appropriate course of action on the part of the organization and also to suggest about the type of media coverage, promotional strategy, booking of venue and about other aspects related to the event planning.

EVENT CHARGES

The event charges are required to be fixed keeping in view the economic and social standards of clients as well as employees, failing which one is likely to face challenges which might have never expected. In all business or profession the objective is to make a sale, which would result in the betterment of the organization. An event organization depends on the clients for whom it works. After all it gets payment from them in exchange of the services as expert rendered to them. The common aim of both the event management organization and the client is to earn and grow. Now event management organization can charge wishfully from the client in exchange of the services rendered by it. While charging the client any fee for the services rendered to the company, one has to justify its demand. Every good effort on its part, helps an organization to achieve the purpose of developing good relation with both internal and external public.

While quoting any cost to the client, each organization evaluates the bases on which it wants to charge an amount from its client. There should be an understanding, image management and confidence which are based on experience and knowledge. The objective in the event management industry is not merely to promote the organization, but to develop the business and offer expert services to as many clients as possible. A strategic thinking based on an overall assessment of various factor are the guiding principle of the decision making in how an organization is going to charge from its clients. There are pros and cons to the various methods, but they all serve a purpose in tailing an organization about whom it will be doing business with, for the planners. Though the client and the event planner are different entities, both have the same goal and objectives to stage a successful event. Any promotional campaign must at the first instance clearly set out its objectives. It must also decide the areas to be covered and the people or the section of the community to be reached.

Success of an event brings the client further closer to the goal the organization intended to achieve, whereas for the event planner success means that they are running a profitable business. Both the client and the event planner want the event to be successful as both of them want to get maximum benefit from the event. For the event charges, a balance between payment for expertise and getting an economical deal is required.

Both the parties have commercial and individual identity angles. The planner seeks to maximize profits and client seeks to keep the cost to the minimum. Sometimes striking a deal which safeguards interest of both parties may be difficult as well as manipulative. The fee system in the event industry is similar to that of in advertising industry. An advertising agency receives a fifteen per cent straight commission from the media for advertisement placed by the agency. The service charges system is some what similar for the charges from the clients in the event planning business.

While quoting the amount to be charged the event planner usually follows the following four different ways. These are:

1. Percentage of the Total Event Cost;
2. Flat Fee;
3. Package Price;
4. Hourly Rate

Percentage of the Total Event- Cost

The traditional fifteen percent commission remains a form of agency income especially for modestly budgeted accounts. Clients and agency may agree to a relationship in which the rate is fixed at less than fifteen percent. This generally applies to large budget accounts, the larger the budget, the lower the rate for the agency. Event planning companies do not always charge the same percentage for each type of event they do or to every client. The percentage charge may vary as it is based on different factors. The type of event has an impact on the percentage charged because different types of projects require different level of expertise and can involve the additional expense of key people such as creative directors, producers, art designers, writers that may not normally be required. So it should be clearly understood by the event planner as well as client that just by the nature of their design and the elements that are included, event might be much more labor intensive or demand special attention.

So event planning agencies come up with "creative costing" methods that can provide them additional revenue, such as listing the hotel rate so that it appears to be so when they are receiving the commission being paid either directly to them or sub-contracted from their payment to the hotel. Planners need to provide value for money and clients willing to pay for professional help. Event planners charge the amount which they think is justified for the services they would be providing to the clients, where as the client who hires the event companies wants to nickel and dying their suppliers and those involved in the planning process are short listed. They also change suppliers very often in search of the best deal, not the quality service. Contracting the cheapest service provider may not prove the least expenses at the end of the day.

But both the client and event planner must think that they can not compromise on the standard of event planning and coordination. In case of event charges based on the percentage of the total event costs, it is necessary to clearly define exactly what cost will be covered under the banner. All programme elements are listed and then percentage charges are applied. What is included and what not included in the event charges needs to be clearly mentioned in the contract papers.

If the event planners and the clients are looking to build long-term relationship, they can offer a preferred percentage rate on their actual event charges, to selected clients. This is usually done in case of signing a long term contract say for three to five years for some specific business or conference or all of their business and social event planning needs, during the period. When the client received a preferred fee rate both the client and the planner are making a contracted commitment to do business together on long term basis, both parties involved recognize the benefits equally.

Some clients need more handholding, more personal involvement and contact. Other clients require multiple meetings that continuously pull staff away from the task at hand which is not favorable for the event planner as well as the client in long-term. In such cases time consumed must be compensated, if it is above and beyond what is deemed reasonable.

Flat Fee

Some clients and the planners may consider opting for a flat fee against the one based on percentage. Event charges based on percentage can exceed a fair rate of return if the budget is in the upper limits. Some events can be intricate and take thousands of man-hour to coordinate and produce, but other may just sound as complicated to someone who is uninformed. Clients unfamiliar with what is required to produce a custom audio- visual presentation, for example, could easily end up excessive amounts in fees if they are not dealing with a reputed event planner.

Every event is organized with mutual agreement between the event planner and the client, both the parties are required to maintain the quality of the event. At times in the process of event planning, decision makers make some changes, budgets are increased, items are taken out or added in a variety of things and when the costing is redone, the issue of rates may come under scrutiny. Clients preferred the flat rate to get the maximum from the event planner by paying the flat fee. Event planners prefer to offer the flat fee to client with big budget and big brand name, in hope to not work hard for getting media coverage.

Package Price

Event planners may also offer a package price. One method is to simple list all inclusive in one price that also includes the management fees. The inclusions are detailed but the individual pricing is not broken down. Taxes and service charges are often listed separately, but this is only to allow the planner to advertise a visually attractive price to consumers. In package price, each change involves a complete a new costing for every alternation. Before entering into any agreement, the event planner and the client should agree to the terms and conditions and the plan of action for the event before. Only after this the event planner should start working on the plan.

Hourly Rate

For an event planning agency it is impossible to offer services on hourly basis. Freelancers commonly charge an hourly rate rather than a set fee. Freelancers are generally sub-contracted by public relations agencies to assist them in event planning and operations. Corporations may also hire them for special in-house projects. The rate and payment schedule is negotiated up-front, the total number of hours to be used to complete the task, remains the unknown factor.

A planner may be brought in on consultancy basis, when a company such as an advertising or public relations agency receives a request to plan a large scale event for one of their clients. A planner may be contracted to act as a consultant under the public relations agency or an event management agency. Consultants are responsible for drafting event strategies and communication strategies in coordination with other experts involved in the process of event planning. Expert advice is considered to be helpful at all stages of event planning. If the event works go well, certain event companies may also like to enter into contract with consultants for future events that they may organize for the present and in future as well. In addition to the hourly rates charged by free lancer, other expenses could include mileage and parking, if required to commute the official site of the event. However these items need to be agreed upon and mentioned clearly in the contract papers.

SUGGESTED QUESTIONS

1. What is the importance of creative visualization in event management?
2. What is creativity and how does creativity comes about?
3. What are the different theories about underlying mechanism in creativity?
4. What are the different elements of an event team?
5. What are different methods of designing an event and its various elements?
6. How are event charges decided?

3

Event Proposal, Feasibility and Financial Management

Event Proposal

Preparation of an event proposal is the first step of an event management. Proposal is considered to be the most important from planning an event to making any changes in the objectives of the company. A proposal is a roadmap on which the entire event management works. Proposal is prepared on concrete facts, presented in a logical sequence in convincing manner. It is prepared and contains sound information based on facts. Once it is prepared and presented, it becomes the backbone of the entire event plan. A proposal is both a creative concept and a plan.

The proposal is the axis of the proposed event around which the entire arrangement revolves. It must meet the requirements of the client in the most economical and professional manner. Every client is looking for an opportunity to gain profitable results and may not feel fully satisfied with the creative concepts or tools used for in presenting the proposal in a professional and impressive way. Multinational organizations usually hire special event management agencies for launching an event. Like other professional bodies such as Public Relations, Event Industry also follows certain code of ethics as prescribed by the International Special Events Society (ISES).

Proposal Request: The proposal is prepared in response to receiving a request from the prospective client intending to hold an event. Proposal request may be made by the professional expertise of the client. But some of these requests are found vague with only outlines of what the client would like to see. The proposal is an important tool in the hands of an event agency as it helps to secure a new client. The success comes in a hard way in event industry.

The proposal may come in a brief formal request or in a much more detailed request. The request may include the type of events the organization organized during the last three years and what they would like to include new things and changes and make alterations. They would also include the budgeted amount under which it is to be worked out. The proposal must clearly mention what can be achieved and what not under the budget fixed for the purpose. The account executives are trained persons and would like to present their proposal at the earliest possible. Event proposal is an effort on the part of event agency to sell its image and its capability to perform professionally. The most successful in achieving sales goals take their own time to qualify the inquiry before they begin.

Planners are required to take time to review it with experts in the agency, otherwise they are at a risk of wasting time, energy and money on something that may be entirely off the work. Before planning and preparing the proposal the event management agency must seek detailed information related to the proposed event from the client. The client should also give appropriate time to the event planner so that the event agency can prepare and present the best possible options for considerations.

The planners also must request for a qualification meeting with the client in order to demonstrate that they won't proceed without understanding the needs of the client. Though now-a-days client is least interested in the way event agencies perform its jobs and professional ethics have no place in Indian industry. The client, especially the multinational, just want maximum coverage. And those who are ready to provide what they are looking for, will be rewarded. It is the responsibility of the client also to give opportunity to such agencies which follow the ethical way of work and are capable of providing the results.

Approval Meeting: Proposal request are the starting point for the planning process. In spite of a good professional level of the client proposal request, it does not provide sufficient detail and information, enough to help and facilitate the event planner bring in strategic event planning strategy and technique required to meet the event objectives.

It is wise on the parts of planners to arrange a face to face meeting with the representative of the client to seek additional information-clarifications required, if any. Also to put across their views and know the views of the client and arrive at a conclusion about what actually are required to be done. Even dozens of correspondence from both sides can not clarify what half-an hour's meeting can do. It is also wise on the part of the event planner to remain always prepared for making alterations in the plan while discussing the business. Event planners while discussing the event proposal should always be equipped with a backup plan in hand and place the same for consideration, in case the clients reject the proposal. It is the responsibility of the event planner to brief the client about own views while presenting the proposal, in case the client disapproves or gives different opinion on any particular issue.

There are a number of topics to be discussed in the approval meeting:

(i) Credential of the client;
(ii) Motivation behind holding the event;
(iii) List of social class of guests in the event;
(iv) List of guest of the event;
(v) Type of events done by them before;
(vi) Names of places where they have done the event;
(vii) Types of event elements included;
(viii) Favorable and unfavorable elements from client's prospective;
(ix) The actual cost of the event, incurred;
(x) Types of services to be offered to the client and the cost to be incurred;

(xi) Strategy to be adopted to make the event successful;
(xii) Draft of legal contract for an agreement with the client;

Promotion of the Event: Promotion and Public Relations are a crucial part of the marketing of any event. Broadly, the aim of a promotional strategy is to ensure that the consumer makes a decision to purchase and follow up the action. It is essential to turn attention into action, and this step is often the biggest obstacle of a promotional campaign. Event promotion involves communicating the image and content of the event programme to potential audience.

Some of the elements involved in the promotion of the events include the following:

- Image Building/Branding;
- Advertising;
- Publicity; and
- Public Relations.

Image and logo are closely linked and they are referred to together as "Branding". A consistency and theme must be obtained. There should be no conflict over the use or the positioning and size of logos. The design must meet the needs of all stakeholders, as well as appealing to the event audience.

Advertising: Advertising is another important element of the promotional strategy. It may be through any one or all the following media of communication:

- Print;
- Radio;
- Television;
- Direct Mail;
- Outdoor Media like hoarding, billboards, neon-signs;
- Brochures/Folders/ Leaflets;
- Internet.

Publicity: Publicity for an event can be secured through a careful publicity campaign. This involves distribution of press-releases containing detailed information about the intended event and also after its conclusion. The aim of the press release is to stimulate media interest in the event and achieve positive and cost effective publicity.

Public Relations: The role of Public Relations is to manage the image of the organizations and of the event in the minds of the audience and the public. They provide to the media up-to-date information along with photographs and background information. Media briefing may also be conducted before and during the event. High profile people such as a celebrities, entertainers and athletes can enhance the publicity. An incident reporting system needs to be in place so that senior members of the event management team are fully informed, including the Public Relations manager. It may be necessary to prepare a press release or to remain prepared to face media representatives if any such incident happens. The role of public relations can be highly sensitive one and in some situation highly professional as well.

Another more positive role of public relations is the entertainment of guests and VIPs attending the event, in some cases from other countries. Also to remain attentive to the needs and expectations of the guests, informative and helpful as host, pro-active in meeting the required protocol and able to converse with them easily.

FEASIBILITY OF THE EVENT

Feasibility of an event can be assessed after careful analysis of the feasibility of an event and detailed analysis of potential risk. Anticipating risk and planning preventive measure can reduce the liability of the event management company. Before undertaking the job the event management agency must have a positive answer to the question "Is this event feasible" ?

Keys to Success

The following keys to success were developed by Errst and Young, adviser to the Olympic Games, the emmy awards and the PGA Tours (Catherwood and Kirk,1992):

- Is event a good idea?
- Do we have the skills required to plan an run the event?
- Is the host community supportive?
- Do we have the infrastructure in the community?
- Can we get a venue at a price we can afford?
- Will the event attract an audience?
- Will it attract media support?
- Is it financially viable?
- Are the success criteria reasonable?

In addition to nine question listed, there is the question of risk management as one of the important concern for the event manager. Events can go right, but they can also go wrong. For an event manager to be involved in an event that goes wrong is not only carrier limiting but also catastrophic. The alternative opportunity to run another event may not occur and the concerned event manager will have to seek for alternative carrier. The risk for most business operation is spread more evenly than it is for the event manager or the event management organization. A bad day's business for a company that trades throughout the whole year, is not as catastrophic as a bad day's business for a one day event.

Is the Event a Good Idea?

Although the question appears quite simple, there are many event management teams that ask this question more and more frequently event draws near. The measurement of public support for the Commonwealth Games, 2010 will be the organizer's expectations about robust sales of ticket. No doubt the organizers will be asking the preceding questions many times in the months leading to the event and hopefully before they made the bid only to doubts resolve at the last minute when record sales of ticket where reported. It is a major question any city bidding for the Olympic Games or the Commonwealth Games and one that needs to be carefully considered at an early stage of the process.

Do We Have the Skills?

Criticism of the Delhi Commonwealth Games 2010 is made on wide scale and is being documented by the media in the years and the months leading to the games. However, any doubts could be resolve only when the game take place and prove to be an outstanding success, demonstrating that the required range of skills did exist, as being claimed by the Organizing Committee. If, however, the concept was developed as a charitable fund-raising event, it would be necessary to carefully consider the ongoing time and commitment required by the volunteers to sustain the event periodically and on a sustained basis, till the conclusion of the event.

Is the Host Community Supportive?

Some cities and states tend to field ambivalent about hosting a Commonwealth Game or an Olympic Games. The citizens of Delhi may vote against holding the proposed Olympic Games in 2020 in Delhi, if given an opportunity to do so, in view of the hardships being faced by them due to ongoing construction work for the Commonwealth Game 2010. The people as a whole must commit to significant expenditures and inconvenience, and some business and residents undoubtedly have the experience of negative consequences. For example there are constant complaints about the road work being done leading to the Commonwealth Games 2010. With a new road improvement work being done to highways, and construction of connecting roads from the games village to different stadium, the roads were in turmoil for a number of months leading to the Commonwealth Games. There was the belief among some people including Union Ministers that the funds could have been better spent on schools and hospitals with urgent problems. However those with an interest in the tourism industry and an understanding of the economic potential of the game were far more positive. An analysis of the community support must take the opinions of all such stakeholders into the account.

Do We Have the Infrastructure in the Community?

The infrastructure required for an Olympic Games or a Commonwealth Game is enormous, shortage of room-accommodation, poor transportation and parking facilities in Delhi are being given as examples. Bid cities generally have to make commitment to infrastructure development in order to win the Games and are then faced with the issue of the viability of these venues after the games are over. Transportation and parking facility are generally important considerations.

Can We Get a Venue at a Price We Can Afford?

For most event organizers the cost of venue rental is a key consideration. Many are tempted to save money by renting tents or canopies and using temporary accommodation but this method can prove a false saving, since the décor lighting, electricity and catering are generally more expensive and more risky. The benefits of function room include tried and tested facilities, safety plans, insurance and a number of other features. The expertise of venue managers can contribute to the technical success of an event. The location and the cost of venue can cast great impact pricing and promotion of an event, specially an entertainment event.

The cost of the venue also depends on the time for which it is required. In some cases the time needed for setting up and dismantling is likely to cost higher than expected rental cost. Goldblatt (1997) refers to these as time, space, temp laws, pointing out that the actual physical space governs the time required. He cites the example of a Superbowl at which 88 pianos had to be removed into the field during half an hour's/time. Loading area access and storage are other considerations. But security is of special concern because high-priced items can get missing.

Despite the fact that such venues remain a lasting legacy for the host city, their long term financial viability is always a matter of concern.

Will the Event Attract Audience ?

The location of the event venue or site is crucial for attracting the numbers of audience required to make the event successful. Identifying the audience is a key issue for event manager in planning an event. Market research into current trends is essential for event feasibility planning.

Will the Event Attract Media Support ?

Media support is essential for the success of any event. Whether the event will attract national and international attention, as in case of the Commonwealth Games or in the Olympics or a local television/radio station or a home town newspaper, depends on the type of event, successful organizers take a look at the different media facilities that are available. They try to determine which media facilities their possible audience use to get their news. For example, if the event is children's fare, then the organizers should try to determine which television and radio stations, newspapers and magazine the parents are most likely to use in that community. Press releases, guest appearances and even advertisement should then be targeted through those media. Stories and images, with a focus on the value of the community can stimulate both media and community interest in the event. A special feature, including advertisements by exhibitors, would be well received at the local level.

Is the Event Financially Viable ?

An event that is financially viable and that brings benefit to the community can outweigh most of the objections. One that is not viable will have a short life span. The Kisan Mela (Farmer's Fair) would not be likely to make profits or generate substantial charitable funds but it might contribute to community spirit and also provide intangible benefits to the local population, specially farmers and other members of the farming community. For example it might enhance the agricultural productivity and the reputation of local agricultural products, and attract, in turn, investment in the farm grown products. Fees charged from the venders would need to cover maximum expenses incurred on the event, since there would be no charge to visitors.

For most event the decision as to what price is to be charged from visitors and spectators, and when the decision is made, is critical. Ticket can not be sold the day after an event is over, nor can the merchandise that was produced for the event. The failure to sell T shirts, caps, CDs etc will mean lost revenue for the event. For both these reasons, the decision on price and the timing of this decision are extremely important that the event expenses reach a viable level.

For the event manager, a careful attention to budgeting will provide a reasonably accurate idea of the costs involved in running the event and this is essential in making a decision about the charge for tickets. Before ticket prices are fixed, it is necessary to understand the local market and the consumer's perceptions regarding value for money and their paying capacity. However in cases like exhibitions, the price charged for exhibiting is based on the cost of staging exhibition and the likely number of exhibitors. For non profit events, financial decisions involve keeping within the budget. When a client is paying for the staging of an event, the event management agency will develop a budget for the event based on the expectations from the client about the benefits expected from the event. Often the event management agency charges a fee and the client is responsible for the cost of the budgeted items and any variations.

Are the Success Criteria Reasonable ?

The criteria on which the success of event is judged vary from event to event. The Commonwealth Games or the Olympic Games are generally judged on feed back from the national and international audience. The feedback on the continuing sponsorship of the games depends on the response of the world television audience. This is one of the most relevant criteria for the success of any such mega-event.

The Kisan Mela could encourage local growers to develop entrepreneurial skills and to produce and market a different product and cash crops. This has already been done by many sugar mill owners and also by fruit and vegetables mega marts. They have even started contract farming for particular fruits and vegetables during a particular season in a fixed quantity and predetermined prices. For this they are paying sufficient amount to farmers to produce and supply fruits and vegetables at predetermined prices.

A wedding is an interesting event to analyze in terms of success. Its success can be judged on various criteria those of the bride groom, the parents or guests. Then just about everyone attending the event has his own point of view about the décor and color scheme. The criteria for the success of the event need to be established before the event takes place, as it is against these that the feasibility of the event is analyzed.

What Are the Risks ?

This final question is the most important of all, because failures, and even fiasco, are always possible.

The first step is to reveal all of the possible risks associated with an event, and then ranking them. Risks may include the following:

- Heavy weather, wind, and/ or rain
- Flooding
- Fire
- Collapse of buildings or temporary structures
- Accidents involving workers and/or the event audience
- Crowd control
- Security of participants and VIPs
- Food poisoning
- Breakdown in water supply or power supply

The second step is the contingency planning, in order to deal with potential risks. And the third step is that policies and procedures must be put in place to deal with every possible eventuality.

The IACC (International Association of Conference Centers) has set international standards for operations, facilities, equipment, and management for small-to medium-sized conference centers (20 to 50 people), and many conference venues around the country are adopting these as a benchmark. This type of accreditation is reassuring for the event organizer and an excellent method of reducing many of the most common risks. Links to this association are listed at the end of the chapter.

To briefly summarize, the aim of the event organizer is to improve feasibility and to reduce risk.

The SWOT, Analysis

It is traditional, and important, to do a SWOT analysis for every event. This involves analyzing the Strength, Weaknesses, Opportunity and Threats (SWOT) of the event are the event concept.

S Strengths are the internal strengths of the organization, for example, the enthusiasm and commitment of volunteers, the specialist knowledge of the lighting engineer or the wide range of products available for planning themes and décor.

W Weaknesses are the internal weaknesses of the organization for example, the skills and the knowledge of the management committee or their lack of availability for the meetings.

O Opportunities are the external favorable things that may occur, such as new sponsorship or unexpected positive publicity.

T Threats are also external competition, poor publicity and poor crowd behavior, all be classified as threats.

Essentially, the idea of improving the feasibility of an event is to improve the strengths of the organization and the concept and to maximize the opportunities. Likewise, acknowledging potential weaknesses and dealing with them will minimize the risks. Assessing the potential threats and introducing contingency plans to circumvent them will also improve the feasibility of the event.

EVENT PROPOSAL-AT A GLANCE

Event Description

- Event name
- Event type
- Location of event
- Date (s) of the event
- Duration/timing of the event
- Event overview and purpose/concepts
- Aims and objectives of the event

Event Management

- Management responsibility
- Major stakeholders and agencies
- Physical requirements- Venue-Route for streets events-Event map-Event layout
- Audience
- Impact- Social- Environmental- Economic

Approvals and Consultation

- State and central government
- City or Municipal Corporation
- Roads and traffic authority
- Police
- Security
- Environmental
- Liquor licensing/ Excise
- Building
- Health
- Insurance.

Marketing

- Competitive analysis

- Market analysis-customer segmentation-Meeting audience needs-Consumer decision making- price and ticket programme
- Advertising and promotion-Messages-Media- Budget
- Public Relations- Press releases-Media briefing
- Marketing evaluation

Financial Control

- Capital and funding requirements
- Fees
- Costs
- Control systems
- Taxation
- Profit and loss statements
- Cash flow analysis

Risk Management

- Identifications of risks and hazards
- Assessment of risks and hazards
- Management of risks and hazards
- Incident Reporting

Event Staging

- Theme
- Décor-Layout-Entertainment- Special effects-Lighting-Sound
- Services-Electricity-Water-Transportation- Traffic management-Street closer-Diversions-Support Vehicles-Parking-Disability access- Security
- Catering-Providers- Facilities- Food safety plans
- Waste and environmental management-Toilets-Waste management, Recycling-Noise-Water pollution
- Cleaning

Staffing

- Selection and recruitment
- Training
- Briefing
- Industrial relations
- Recruitment of volunteers

Safety and Security

- Safety of the event audience
- Safety and security of the artists, VIPs, etc
- Communications-Meetings-Reporting relationships-Emergency reporting relationships-Communication methods
- Emergency access and emergency management-First aid

Operational Plans

- Policies- Complaints- Crowd control
- Procedures and check lists
- Performance standard (commensurate with objectives)
- Contingency plans-Weather-Electrical supply-Fire-Accident-Crowd control-Delay or cancellation-Bomb threats, etc
- Logistics- Setup-Structures and Facilities-Lighting-Sound

Evaluation

- Post- event evaluation- Objectives-Measures-Analysis-Report

FINANCIAL MANAGEMENT

Financial viability of the event proposal is always the core factor in assessing the feasibility of any such proposal. Long term financial results are always an important consideration in any event management. The aim of any financial management is for all expenses to be recouped at the time of the event. Profit is the main motive of the most of the organizers in any event. Not all events are profit oriented.

At times, the promotion for a new product would be major marketing initiative with the expectation for long-term return through sales. Similarly a party or a celebration is paid for the client.

Good financial management by an event company will ensure that quote given to the client at the beginning will at least cover the expenses incurred in staging the event and hopefully make a profit for the company.

A good financial management requires keep in consideration while finalizing the proposal for an event:

- Is the aim of the event to make a profit ?
- How much will the event cost ?
- What are the revenue sources ?
- What is the cash flow situation ?
- What control system will be needed to avoid fraud ?

BUDGET

Preparing a budget for an event is the part of the initial planning and feasibility report. A budget includes projected revenue and expenditure and an estimate of the net profit from the proposed event can be ascertained. It is a plan based on accurate quotes from all contractors and suppliers. A careful research keeping into consideration all these elements can ensure that new expenses have not been overlooked. It provides guidelines for approving expenditure and ensuring that the financial aspects of the event remain on track. Budget is the part of event proposal or the feasibility report or the basis of quote by the event management company to the client. The budgets vary in the number of expense and revenue items, though the general principle remains the same. There is a difference between the fixed cost (which do no alter) and variable cost (varying with the size of event audience).

Management Fees

In many cases an event organizer charges a management fee to over-see an event. As a ballpark figure for planning purposes this fee is generally in the range of 10 to 15 per cent of total cost Larry Jaeger, president of Events Xtraordinaire, the industry has gotten a bit more competitive, so there are situations in which an event planner may look at a business as an opportunity and get more aggressive on fees. Jaeger also reports that any fees in addition to what is specified in the project or any project that are smaller in nature, are billed on a per-hour consultation fee, depending on the region and venue of the event. An event might have low budget it still might require considerable time and effort in organizing it. The end of the range, 10 per cent, may not always cover management cost. In those cases, an event planner may opt for the hourly consultation fees.

Prior to contracts being signed, the event organizer should work out the tasks involved in the management, allocate staff to various roles and determine their pay rates to come up with a more accurate management cost and the management fee to be charged accordingly. In some situation the event organizer might involve himself in a collaborative entrepreneurial arrangement with the client. In such case the management fee is based on total income earned. If the management fee is charged, the client will be responsible for all pre-events payments to venue owners and subcontractors. The fee is charged for the management and coordination of the event by the event organizer and also for their expertise in converting the concept to execution.

Contingent Expenditure

Most event budgets include contingent funds for unexpected expenses. This contingent fund may range from 5 per cent to 10 per cent of the total cost. The variation depends on number of unknown variables or uncertain costs.

Break-Even Point

The event organizer has to estimate the number of ticket that need to be sold in order to meet expenses, to work out the break-even point.

These expenses include both fixed cost and variable costs. Fixed costs include licensing fees, insurance premium, administrative costs, rent of office accommodation, advertising cost and fees paid to the artist. The fixed costs normally do not vary and if the size of the event audience increases, the additional costs are often called overheads. Variable costs increase as the size of the audience increases. Variable costs would escalate if the number of persons attending the conference increased, if the food and beverage costs are included in the conference package. The basis of calculating the break even-point is to compare the total revenue with the total expenditure, and if both are at the same amount, the break-even point has been achieved. In case of revenue exceeding the expenditure, it is profitable and if the expenditure exceeds the revenue, it is a case of loss.

In the case of an exhibition the organizer would be using the budget to establish how many exhibitors would be needed to reach to the break-even point, the price charged for exhibiting could be quite low, if there were a large number of exhibitors participating. On the other hand the price charged would have to be kept high if there were only a few exhibitors, in order to meet the budget. However this will also be guided by the capacity of the market to bear the maximum price and at a minimum level at which the event becomes viable. This process of analyzing ticket prices, fees charged and the break even point is the essence of the financial decision-making process.

Cash Flow Analysis

Monthly expenses and projected revenue need to be entered into spreadsheet to find out how the cash flow could have been managed. It has been a common happening in the event industry that a fund crisis has arisen. Capital is required to set up any business as well as in the event industry. It has also been observed that planning phase is often long and the period for collection of revenue very short. During the long planning period cost will be incurred and had to be paid long before there is an opportunity to recoup that money from revenue collection. In an event industry it is possible that all revenue will be collected on one day from the sales of tickets, but after a long period of planning, say, after a year or so. This outcome in the event industry is in contrast to every day business in which there is a more even cash flow, almost on daily basis.

In some instances the client would be paying certain amounts in advance for the event, generally depending on the negotiation. But the payment of balance amount may not be made to the event management agency before the conclusion of the event, in most cases generally at least after a month or more after the event. Ideally, a significant establishment fee, preferably complete up-front payment should be negotiated to tide over the cash-flow problems.

During the long planning period, the normal expenses include salaries to the staff, office expenses, security deposits and up-front payments to subcontractors for catering and equipment rents. The gap between the expenditure and the income during the period results in the cash short fall.

Profit and Loss Account

The profit and loss account statement is a list of revenue, expenditure and net profit/loss of an organization during a specific period. In many cases the profit and loss account statement is prepared after the event. In an ideal situation, the profit and loss account statement would tally the budget. The budget is the plan and if every thing went according to the plan this outcome would be reflected in the profit and loss account statement. In the event industry the budget is generally prepared before the event and the profit and loss account statement is prepared after the event. In contrast, in most of other business operations, budgets and profit and loss account statement are prepared regularly. In an event management company, a profit and loss account statement would be done for an event similarly and for on going events collectively being organized by the company, during a certain fixed period. Otherwise each event could be shown as a different cost unit.

Gross revenue is the total revenue earned before the deduction of any costs. This is similar to the concept of gross wages, the amount paid to the recipient before all shorts of deduction such as income tax, PF and other compensation to worker before it reached his pocket. The first item on the profit and loss account statement is the most important source of revenue in case of sales of tickets and the payment made by a single client, if the case be so. It is, after all, the predominant source of revenue.

Gross profit is the gross revenue minus the cost of goods which is also known as direct cost. For example, if the gross revenue from an event was Rs 1,00,00,000 and direct costs of Rs 52, 00,000 were deducted, the result would be a gross profit of Rs 48,00,000. The costs of goods sold are those that relate directly to the revenue earned. They might include the cost of the rent for the event venue, payment made to labors and rent amount paid for the equipment after calculating the gross profit and deducting the overhead costs, such as administrative cost and the amount of rent paid to hire the office accommodation, say of Rs 20,00,000 the event company would be left with operating profit of Rs 28,00,000, finally, the net profit is the profit of the company after deduction of all other cost and taxes.

Profit and Loss Account Statement

Gross Revenue	Rs 1,00,00,000	
Less Cost of goods sold	Rs 52,00,000	
Gross Profit		**Rs 48,00,000**
Less administrative and other overhead cost	Rs 20,00,000	
Operating Profit		**Rs 28,00,000**
Less other Income/ Expenses	Rs 5,00,000	
Profit Before Tax	Rs 23,00,000	
Less Tax	Rs 15,00,000	
		Rs 8,00,000

Balance Sheet

The balance sheet gives an idea of what a particular business companies is of worth at a certain point of time. On the other hand, profit and loss account statement gives the results for a given period of time such as for a financial year. The balance sheet shows what the financial result would be if all outstanding bills for the amount incurred by the owners of the business on acquired and the revenue generated after every thing were sold (the assets minus the liabilities). The result shown is the equity of the owner in the business.

Financial Control Systems

A Financial control system should have checks and balances to make sure that:

- Purchases and other expenses made are duly approved;
- Goods and services meet specification;
- Payment is approved;
- All payments meet be accounted for;
- All incoming revenue is duly checked and deposited in the account;
- Total revenue earned be recorded correctly;
- All transactions are recorded;
- All tax requirement are met;
- Financial matters are reported correctly to the stakeholders.

All purchases must be approved and a requisition form is used for this purpose so that the manager would have the opportunity to approve costs incurred by employees. Once, goods are sold and services provided, it must be checked to ensure that they meet the specification before the bills are paid. The authority to make purchases to record and physically verify the goods and also to pay the bills, in the same hand may encourage fraud.

Major community-wide events with multiple objectives are being staged and also well managed financially.

Panic Payments

The problem of panic payments is not limited to the event industry, but in this industry inflated panic prices are often paid in an ideal situation, the event manager has sewn up all quotes and the budget is fixed long before the event. But there are a few unforeseen circumstances and this may also happen in the case of budget also.

In reality Murphy's Law dictates that something will always go wrong. As the closer it is to the event, the more difficult it is to negotiate a reasonable price for what one requires to put it right. Any last minute crisis could easily lead to a price with a high premium, which is termed as panic payments. Careful planning and detailed contracts negotiated well in advance can prevent any situation of a panic payment, from occurring.

So it is the best practice to develop the budget prior to an event and to must anticipate all revenues and expenditure. Necessary step should be taken to finalize the contracts as early as possible to insure that expenses do not exceed budget forecasts. The event manager needs to take into account the cash-flow situation in the lead up to an event. Reporting systems need to be in place to make available complete and accurate records for the final post-event report.

Planning, Budgeting and Reporting Process

Event Planning

Budget

Expenditure | Revenue

Cash Flow Analysis

Profit and Loss Account | Balance Sheet

Event Evaluation Report

SUGGESTED QUESTIONS

1. How is an event proposal made?
2. What is the role of promotion and Public Relation in the marketing of any event?
3. What are the main elements involved in promotion of an event?
4. How would you assess the feasibility of an event?
5. What can be the possible risks associated with an event?
6. Draw an event proposal-at a glance.
7. What is the importance of financial viability of any event proposal?

4

Event Sponsorship

Concept of Sponsorship

Sponsorship is one of the most common funding sources for staging an event. In some cases, the sponsor may provide cash to support the event in exchange for increased profile and sales of the sponsor's products. In other cases, the sponsors provide "value in kind." In this case the sponsor will provide free goods and services. Some sponsors use an event to promote a new product, and the whole event is aimed at developing customer awareness and loyalty. But in all these cases, the marketing messages must be consistent with the event and must be clear to the audience.

Sponsorship is one of the most powerful positioning tools available to a business. The sponsor identifies with the event mainly through the use of its name and logo and expects a return on the investment. Sponsorship is the means to bring a company or its product to the attention of the consumers. Advertising can provide information on the quality, characteristic, price and performance of the product and is use as a marketing tool to communicate to the consumer in a direct way. Sponsorship should be seen as an effective tool of communication for reaching across the borders. It is essential to evaluate both the profile and sales of the sponsor along with other sponsorship objectives, after the event. It may help to evaluate if the sponsorship has been successful.

Sponsorship is simply another tool in the hands of PR experts who is a contact man between the internal and external public organizations. Though in Indian situation, PR experts are not given appropriate importance by the management who treats them as mere press agents or lobbyists. But the attitude of management is fast changing and demand for communication experts in the extensive competitions due to globalization of economy are the main reason for this change. Sponsorship should not be considered as donation given to create a warm feeling about any particular individual or an organization. It adds value and gives access to a target audience and not solely for corporate social responsibility. Sponsorship is a relatively passive form of communication. It may not work effectively if not planed and executed in a professional manner. Supporting a local community event as occasion, can make difference in the images of a company among both the internal and external publics of the organization. It also helps in presenting the business in a desired light.

Don't underestimate the value of local events and local opportunities. We read so much about the multi-million dollar deals that it's easy to forget that there are many small deals such as $ I,500, $3,500 and $ 10,000 sponsorships. These can be as simple as vertical street banners, which offer great exposure for a very inexpensive cost per thousand, to title sponsorship of a local parade or festival. This association can be very powerful because it is perceived as an endorsement of the brand by an independent third party. Consumers are aware of the costs of sponsorship but the message retained is more subtle than that from the more overtly paid for advertisement. As you go through the following ten-step process, you might get a better understanding of how to put together sponsorship offerings, what words to use and how to put together sponsorship offerings, what words to use, and how to price and evaluate, on a post-event basis, what you provided to the sponsor.

Identifying the Sponsor

Before drafting any sponsor, it is necessary to know about your potential sponsor. As an event expert it is your responsibility to strike on every prospective target to get maximum output for turning your event into a success. The more you know about them, you are better prepared to be ready for their question and it will facilitate you to craft a sponsorship offering that mix their specific needs.

There a number of questions to be asked before approaching a potential sponsor:

What are the benefits for the organization?

Will it be a long term alliance with the sponsor?

How much exposure will the sponsor get?

Will the sponsorship be exclusive or associated with other events?

Is there compatibility between the product of the sponsor and the event purpose?

Will there be ambush marketing?

Can the involvement of the sponsor lead to some benefit for the organization in terms of increased profile and increased sales? What are other benefits? Is it possible to build a long-turn association with sponsor and agreement for a period of five-year sponsorship?

Will the logo of sponsor appear on all advertising and will the wining athletes wear the caps of the sponsor when interviewed by the television crews? Will the sponsor have naming rights to the event? Will this sponsor be the only one associated with the event or there be more then one sponsor?

Is there compatibility between the product of the sponsor and the event purpose? Have the potential sponsor's competitor agreed to provide sponsorship and will this arrangement lead to a conflict of interests?

Are there organizations that will attempt to gain advertising mileage sales from the event without any sponsorship or other commitment?

Ultimately, the most important question of all concerns is the benefit of the sponsor from its involvement in the event.. This consideration needs to be negotiated early in the arrangement and a process for measuring sponsor objectives needs to be put in place prier to, during and after the event. At the end of the day, the sponsor needs a report detailing all promotional efforts and the ensuing benefits, as well as photographs and success stories for post-even publicity. If clearly audited, records or professional surveys can demonstrate sponsorship outcomes, renegotiating sponsorship arrangements for subsequent events or for different events will be much easier, since success has been well documented and demonstrated in a tangible way.

Sponsorship Offerings

Now as an event manager you can put together various components of your sponsorship offerings. You can have title, Presenting, associate, product specific and event-specific categories. Of course, the title is the most effective component. As soon as the name of the event is fixed to the sponsor's name, the media has to give the whole title, resulting in exposure for your sponsor.

Media, Retail Partner and Sponsor

Media and retail partners should be treated as all other sponsors, with the same rights and benefits. Your event offers the media an opportunity to increase their non-traditional revenue. Media people can offer their advertisers sampling opportunities, sales opportunity and multiple media exposure through your targeted audience. Many times an advertiser asks for additional merchandising opportunity from the media. Airtime from radio and television could be included in your sponsorship offerings. From print media you are getting valuable ad space to include in sponsorship offering to your potential sponsors. Just you have to ensure that it is always coordinated through you and they are not approaching directly to your sponsor.

A retail partner, whether it be supermarket or a fast food outlet, offers you some additional benefits that can be passed on to your sponsor. You can also approach manufacturer and offer them some of these benefits through a retail outlet. A retail partner offers you a store relationship for various products. Since sponsorship has to become more and more accountable and offer a strong return on investment, this retail relationship is important to ensure the success of your product sponsorship. Again as with the media, treat the retail partner as you would treat a paying sponsor.

Creativity

Your knowledge and research and forethought, provide them the knowledge as to how they can maximize their participation in the event. Make them aware of hospitality opportunity such as rewards for leading sales people, special customer awards and incentives for the trade. Along with offering these ideas you must help the sponsor understand how this sponsorship offers them a great benefit. Also help them create a new and unique way to enhance their sponsorship beyond the event.

Involvement of Sponsor

After going through the sales proceeds you determine their needs and develop a programme to meet those needs. You also determine their level of participation and keep your sponsor involve through out the event. Show them collateral promotional materials while they are being developed. They are also to be kept up-to-date on new sponsor and any new activity or announcement. Walk around with them, show their logo placement, discuss their various banner locations, the quality of the audience and what ever is an appropriate to their participation. Every effort should be made to reinforce this participation as a prelude to renewal.

Post- event Sponsorship Maintenance and Renewal

The Sponsor should be provided with complete documentation of their participation and proper feedback to the client regarding the purposeful utilization of the money spent by sponsor in the event. The feedback material should include all collateral materials, and affidavit of performance from your radio and television partners, press stories, brochures, tickets, banners and any other material that has there company's name or logo prominently displayed or mentioned. The post event report to the sponsor must document the value of all the marketing components they received.

Ultimately, the most important question of all concerns is the benefit of the sponsor from its involvement in the event. This consideration needs to be negotiated early in the arrangement and a process for measuring sponsor objectives needs to be put in place prier to, during and after the event. At the end of the day, the sponsor needs a report detailing all promotional efforts and the ensuing benefits, as well as photographs and success stories for post-even publicity. If clearly audited, records or professional surveys can demonstrate sponsorship outcomes, renegotiating sponsorship arrangements for subsequent events or for different events will be much easier, since success has been well documented and demonstrated in a tangible way.

SPORTS SPONSORSHIP

Sponsorship is a commercial agreement between a company and a sport organization to inter into a joint venture to promote their mutual interest. A sport organization will allow the use of its name in commercial activities to the sponsor in return for a financial contribution. The activities may include:

- Display of the brand name on kit, banners around the venue, advertisement in programmes.
- Personal endorsement of the products of the sponsor by teams or individual member by using their products, kit or equipment.
- Production of joint website or developing close links between separate websites.
- Use of team or individual member in advertisement and other promotional activities undertaken by the brand.

Sponsorship are paid both in cash in kind. In stead of money the sponsor provides equipment, services or management expertise or management expertise fully or partly, as fee for the rights to a sporting activities. Companies may also provide money to the sporting organization in some other ways:

- **Charitable donation:** The company makes the use of donations to be seen as a good corporate citizen
- **Corporate patronage:** The corporate patronage is a halfway house between donations and sponsorship. It is more common in the arts than sports.
- **Corporate hospitality:** It is normally a part of sponsorship package which provide an opportunity to meet customer in informal way and pursue business objectives.
- **Community relations:** It aim is to meet objectives of a company's social or political agenda to improve its images as a corporate citizen or contributor to the economy.

Expectation of the Company from Sponsoring Sport

Sponsors look to sport to add value to their brand positioning. In order to make a brand stand out from the crowd, a sponsor will use sport to create a unique position in the minds of the customers. The sport involve gold medals, world records, and global awareness. A world wide leading brand such as Coca-Cola wants to associate itself with such excellence and ubiquity, so it has chosen the Olympics and the FIFA Football World Cup for its sponsorship. But in order to reinforce its global message, it also supports grass-root sport to localize its image and activities.

Companies use sports sponsorship with certain objectives. Some of them are as follows:

- **Corporate awareness**: Companies seek to put a name in front of the consumer so that he will give it favorable recognition when exposed to other, specific marketing messages.
- **Corporate image**: Companies attempt to create a personality and style which distinguishes a product from another in the market and allows, for example, premium pricing.

- **Customer relations:** Sports sponsorship can open dialogue between companies, showing the sponsor as a global player worthy of recognition and suitable to do business with clients.
- **Employee relations:** Sports sponsorship can encourage company pride and loyalty to help attract and retain staff.
- **Community relations:** Sponsorship can show that a company cares about its community and is present to invest in its future and the welfare of its citizens.

Expectations of a Company from Sponsorship

Sponsors are looking for sports properties that can make a valuable and quantifiable contribution to existing or planned brand communications. A sponsor wants to create activities that are enjoyable and memorable for audiences and participants and provide them occasions to build the brand values and to develop sales opportunities and volumes. The sponsorship must have the same fitting to the brand personality and unique to that brand so that there is no confusion in the mind of consumer.

Sporting event creates thousands of opportunities for exciting and interesting newspaper photographs and television images showing sponsor logos on shirts and banners. Such exposures create brand familiarity for consumers making the logos stand out from competitors when consumers are in the super market or high street looking to spend money. Naming rights for sports venues is now a growing trend. This can backfire if the old name is well recognized and liked.

Some sponsor need to communicate with just a handful of the right people to sell expensive equipment. But above all, the sponsor wants the opportunity to communicate with the customer in the setting where he is enjoying a quality leisure time and is favorably disposed off to any one who makes the occasion possible.

Donations in kinds for Non-profits

Corporations are usually more willing to donate products and services than hard cash to non-profit organizations. Though non-profit organizations are less keen to receive the donations in kind, if carefully managed, donations in kind can do a lot to help non-profit organizations. This may narrow the gap between their aims and resources. The purpose is to create long term partnership between non-profit organizations and donor companies and to make the benefit for both side explicit. This approach gives non-profit organizations more control over what they receive and when they receive it.

Since the gift's cost to the donor is only the production cost, which might be only half of its market price and the market value of the gift may be more than the donations, almost double the value of cash donation from the same donor. More over many corporations have spare capacity that they could put to use for non-profit organizations at a nominal extra costs.

One important benefit that corporations can derive from their gifts in kind is that it enables them to meet and be seen to meet their social responsibilities. Donation in kind can easily and more creatively be communicated externally, than cash, for public relations purposes. Companies can also benefits internally, as employees take greater satisfaction in working for good causes. In this way donors assume the role of supplier and non-profit organization, the role of customers, making them more equal and business like partnership.

The first step in creating mutual value of this kind is to determine the benefits of a donation in kind for the non-profit and the corporate donor. The reward for donor might be positive publicity triggered by agencies working under the media spotlight. An automotive company could gain variable exposure for a new product line/vehicles by donating some vehicles to a relief NGO and may serve the purposes associated with donations in kind. Similarly a timber company might support both a social and environmental cause by providing construction material to help repatriated refugees build new home for themselves.

Local information about human rights and business issue could help a company to act in a socially responsible way, for instance, or the non-profit organizations might offer courses in handling problems that arise when the people of a company work in unfamiliar cultures. It could also help get the media interested in the joint project. For example, a telecom company provides equipment and expertise for an international aid organization's field operations, among other thing, the company installs telecom equipment in emergency where houses have been destroyed. On the one hand it will solve the telecommunication problem of the aid organization, especially in adverse situations, on the other hand it helps to keep up the sprits of employees. Finally feedback information to be provided through field visits must be delivered in cooperation with the people who run the operations, as most donors want the feedback on the progress of a project and their involvement in it.

Developing a Sponsorship Package

Homework: Before seeking sponsorship a sport, it should evaluate what it has to offer, what it can deliver and who it will reach. The organizer also needs details. This is difficult in detail but in broad terms the sponsor's product defines its market: older/younger, affluent/cut-price and so on.

Reasons for partnership: Complete an audit of your sponsorship package. Quantify number of events, participants, spectators and secondary audiences through newspaper, television and radio. Find out how many people play the sport, players and spectators and find out proportions of male, female and ethnic groups. Try and think of ways in which your sponsorship would fit in with other marketing activities of your target companies. Detail the places and times there will be opportunities to display the sponsor's logo, not just at the event but on promotional items, posters, programmes, letterheads or vehicles.

The history of your event organization is important to establish credibility, as is your organizational capacity to deliver. Good financial controls and reporting will encourage sponsor's confidence. If you have been sponsored before, prepare case histories to show activity and results. Learn as much about your target sponsor as you can: use annual reports, company, its management and employees. Finally, put together detailed costing for the venture. These may be tried to reflect levels of expenditure, which would just 'make it happen,' to more sophisticated versions that reach more people with extensive publicity.

Considerations in Commercial Sponsor

Quality vs Quantity: It is better to chose a few targets and work hard in personalizing then giving brief details to a large number of companies.

Personal contact vs General Approach: Personnel contact is responsible for most of the sports sponsorship. Names and functions of the company can be had from local or trade papers. Yellow Pages lists the names of more than 1,000 companies, their interest areas, and contact number. There are a number of trade publications for sponsorship and a number of websites trying to match sponsor and companies. The Sports Sponsorship Advisory Service produces a regular list of sponsor projects that is circulated to companies.

The sporting benefits of the sponsor project are secondary to commercial return available to the sponsor. Companies are now looking for return from investment that is more complex than just an increase in sales. The creation of subsidiary benefit to the sponsor, creates maximum promotional possibilities for the sponsor, allowing them to communicate with several important audiences using the same vehicle.

Birmingham Mid Shires Building Society for example, sponsored a late night football lead that reduced crime figures significantly in there areas. They gained extensive brand awareness and also improved their image as a company that cared about issues that affected families and their homes. Other methods for evaluating the project and reporting back to the sponsor should form a major part of the approach to the sponsor. Concentration on results and delivery from day one will help create a positive response to the proposal.

Running a Sponsorship

It is essential that the sports project runs smoothly, delivers its quality experiences to participants and spectators. But it should not neglect the interest of sponsor. Involvement with the sponsor will maintain interest and demonstrate the value of the investment by the sponsor.

It is necessary to work closely with your sponsor and communicate about the benefit to the sponsors set out in the presentation document. Personal element should be put in to ensure that the sponsor has sufficient tickets for itself and its guests and has a chance to meet participants. The sponsor should be regularly updated about who is doing what, through a clear reporting procedure. Every effort should be made to increase the news worthiness of the event through interesting photo-features and background features. The press, particularly the local press and radio will often run joint promotional activities or act as media partner to the event. If a sponsor has retail outlets-estate agents or builders' society/association, may offer another means of communication through window display, etc.

Sponsor logos must have prime position in any event and in all supporting materials which is a key sponsor requirement. Sports body is an equal partner in the sponsorship and requires its own branding. For the commercial success of the sponsorship, the product of the company needs to be placed as close to the sponsorship as possible. Product displays, sampling opportunities and a sales kiosk at the launch and event venue are also important means for the sponsor to reach its targeted market. Sponsors and organizers should work together to devise longer lasting links, such as discount vouchers for future purchases for those who attend the event. The employees of the sponsor should also be kept informed through the usual channels of the company.

Evaluation of the Sponsorship

Self-evaluation of a project is an essential tool to measure performance against objectives and it also provides a reporting process for the sponsor. It helps the sponsor to know that their investment is valued and the sponsor could know the return they have achieved and help them to sell future sponsorship on the basis of data provided.

Key Principles of Evaluation

- **Measuring participation**: A sponsor wants to reach a specific sector of the market so that data on participants that details age, sex, ethnic origin or social, economic group, can help measure success.
- **Measuring skills**: Achievement of sporting objectives can be measured by noting before and after performance levels of participants. Sports match needs to know this and the data will add the search for future sponsorships.
- **Photographic record**: One of the best ways of showing the impact of a sponsorship is photographs of participants, spectators. Sponsor branding will help and tell the story of your success.
- **Media monitoring**: Collect press clippings, count column centimeters of coverage and the number of photographs and your as well as the interests of clients. Clients know that their entire team can be wiped out any moment they have heard the news and read headlines and so their staff has. We don't like to inter into situations where our whole identity could be questioned and put to test because of mere circumstances. Information related to the following incident appeared in newspaper and other media in India. After going through the news report about this incident, you might be forced, as an event expert, to think about the precautions, an event organizer could have taken to prevent this kind of incident or you might be able to judge the reasons behind this incident.

Fire at wedding kills 54

Srirangam (Tamil Nadu), January 23

Tragedy struck at a wedding ceremony when a fire engulfed the pandal on the first floor of a marriage hall in this temple town, killing 54 persons, including the bride groom and injuring 40, the police said.

Thirty five- year old Jayashri, the bride was down stares awaiting the "muhooratham" when the fire broke out as a video crew tried to fix the plug of a focus lamp that burst due to a short circuit.

The bride groom, 42-year old Guru Raghavendra, working in General Insurance Company was charred to death, the police said over 400 person has gather in the marriage hall, situated on the EVS Street, Ranganagar.

Raju Pillaie, a watch man in the neighboring building said he heard a thud and show smoke emanating from the pandal, which collapsed immediately. "There was suffocating and blinding smoke, and pungent smell, which delayed rescue operations by the people who rushed to the sport," he said. The scenes witnessed thereafter were disturbing and heartening, he said.

As the fire raged, there was stampede, as the guests could not come down due to the narrow stare case, in which an old man was lying unconscious. Many people got stuck in the plastic chairs, which melted in the fire and it was not easy for people to remove them. Many collapsed in the chairs they where occupying.

On lookers found it difficult to console those who had lost several of their kith and kin. The watchman said he saw bodies being removed in three garbage trucks to the hospital.

The stench of burning plastic flesh and ghee lingered in the air for three hours after the fire was doused by members of the public and fire service personnel. Fire service personnel said flesh and hair were found glued to the walls and pillars of the hall plastic materials and asbestos sheets on the sides of the hall added to the intensity of the fire.

There were problems at the government hospital also as the mortuary was full and bodies had to be laid outside, covered with saris. Government hospital officials said 44 bodies, including 23 women, a girl, and a boy, had been identified. Of the 40 injured, 20 suffered third degree burns and there condition was very critical. Some of them where admitted to a nursing home. Top officials, including District Collector Manivasagan, and the IG police, were overseeing the operations. –PTI

The news story gives a vivid hint as to what can happen at any moment of time of any event organized. Event planners have to cross check the resources available to them for making the event successful and hazards free. They could have now realized what rescue operation and emergency measures are required to be kept in 'ready to go' conditions to alleviate the problems to the extent possible.

Another news item appear in both Indian media and the international media about Haj Pilgrimage Stampede in Saudi Arabia: "There were 244 pilgrims who died in the incident in Jamarat and 244 who were injured," pilgrimage affairs and endowments minister Iyad bin Amin Madani said. Among the dead were three Indians. The disaster happened as two million pilgrims, wrapped white robes, flocked to Jamarat Bridge in Mena to throw stones at pillars representing the Devil during Eid. The stampede lasted 27 minutes.

Madani said a huge number of pilgrims had opted to perform the ritual at the same time although the kingdom had been encouraging them two stagger times to prevent stampede. "There were more than four hundred members of people pushing in the same direction (which) resulted in the collapse of those next to the stoning area.... and those behind. That led to panic."

Most of the victims where from inside the Saudi kingdom and that many had not been authorized to participate, he said, adding several of them were carrying personal belongings, which caused obstructions. Madani said another 272 pilgrims had died of natural causes during Haj. He said movement of Jamarat Bridge was well controlled between midnight and 5.30 a.m. on Sunday before the crush. "I assure you that all the preparation are always made, but we don't always know God's intentions," he said.

The devil-stoning is the most animated ritual of the annual pilgrimage and often the most dangerous. Many pilgrims frantically throw rocks, shout insults or hurl their shoes at the pillars—acts that are supposed to demonstrate their deep disdain for the devil. Clerics frown upon such action and say it's un-Islamic.

Such news items are bound to create doubts in the minds of the clients as well as the guests intending to attend an event. For successful completion for any event it is the responsibility of the event manager to make it safe and secure to the extent possible. For safety purposes event planners must consider hiring the services of professional security companies to assess the risk involved in the proposed events. The security experts should assess the risk during the planning process stage itself. The planners should meet the security expert and review the fire and evacuation procedures put in place and the set up for the flow of information and chain of command to meet any such eventuality.

With the increasing importance of safety, the success of the events largely depends upon the safety measures taken and evacuation plan put in place by the event planner. In view of fact that danger and hazards are always a possibility, only a pro-active action can help the event manager to make the event successful in an appropriate manner. Planners are always obliged to put forward best possible suggestion to their clients knowing that every thing has been handle behind the scenes. At times, event planner will be dealing with the rich people who can afford to pay any thing demanded, challenges would be many. The option of organizing theme parties would help these event planners to plan a show hassle free.

SUGGESTED QUESTIONS

1. What do you mean by Event Sponsorship?
2. Sponsorship is one of the most common funding sources for staging an event. Explain in details.
3. How can one identify sponsor?
4. How media retail partners and sponsor are interrelated?
5. How can the participation be reinforced for renewal?
6. How can a sponsor use sport event to create a unique position in the minds of consumers? Give reasons.
7. What does a company expect from sponsorship?
8. What are the key principles of evaluation of the sponsorship?

5

EVENT MARKETING

Event marketing essentially, involves the study of brand character and the creation of an event strategy that gels with it of a client or the planner. In India, however, this has been the functions of the client. But now this function has become a part of event planners in India also. The concept of event is getting attention and the client wants to be associated with the event planners who have the sound backing and vision to promote the business of the clients. In spite of a successful media campaign, there is always a possibility of a shift in media strategy- like changing the media to give a boost to advertising results achieved already from the first phase of the campaign. The advertiser will also benefit from the carry over effects of the television spots that ran during the first phase of the campaign and thus consumers may experience the feeling that advertising for the product has been increased.

Marketing: The Chartered Institute of Marketing defines marketing as "The management process responsible for identifying anticipating and satisfying customer requirements profitability."

Marketing requires co-ordination, planning, implementation of campaigns and a competent manager (s) with the appropriate skills to ensure success. Marketing objectives, goals and targets have to be monitored and met, competitor strategy analyzed, anticipated and exceeded. Through effective use of market and marking research, an organization should be able to identify the needs of the customer resulting in a healthy turn over from the organization.

Philip Kotler defines marketing as "satisfying needs and wants through an exchange process". Within this exchange transaction customers will only exchange what they value (money) if they feel that their needs are being fully satisfied. Clearly the greater the benefit provided the higher transactional value an organization can charge.

MARKETING

Marketing is an important function of management in every organization, be it a government organization, corporate business house or a non profit organizations is involved in the process of marketing.

According to Peter Drucker, "The aim of marketing is to make selling superfluous. The aim is to know and understand the customer so well that the product or service fits... and sells itself." Marketing is a social and managerial process by which individuals and groups obtain what they need and want through creating and exchanging products and value with others.

Marketing management is the process by which marketers achieve the objectives of their organizations. The core of this process is managing level, timing and composition of demand by retaining current customers and also attracting new ones. This is accomplished by developing marketing programs for the target market through the process of analysis, planning implementation and control. Marketing management is the setting of goals considering the resources available with the company and marketing opportunity.

To make an event successful, knowledge of management function is essential. Events are organized to earn foreign exchange, encourage developmental activities, improve local economies and generate employment opportunities. For every event expert it is necessary to understand the basic concept of the management. Event experts need to be trained in the fundamentals of management and they must know how to coordinate marketing policy, process of planning and decision making. They should have also the knowledge of managing finance, budgeting, communication, media management, writing for events, etc. Success of every event depends upon the strategic planning which are based on certain management functions.

Fan Fare is one of America's best examples of an event that grows from strength to strength, gaining in popularity from year to year. It continue to enhance Nashville's Image as a tourist destination the reason for its success has lot to do with marketing and what is known as the marketing mix-the combination of product, price, promotion and place. The choice of messages and the channel of communication are also important for the audience. These factors taken together form the parts of the marketing strategy.

Marketing helps to attract an audience for an event. The event audience makes decisions after weighing the cost and effort to attend against the benefits of attending. An understanding of the decision making processes of the audience is essential for event planner and organizer.

Nature of Event Marketing

Event products generally include a combination of goods and services, and so provide a challenge for those involve in event marketing. There are three features of services marketing; Intangibility, Variability and Inseparability.

The first feature of marketing is its intangibility. The second feature of services marketing is a higher degree of variability in the service provided, as well as in the response to the service provided. The third feature of service marketing is that the service and the service provided are distinguished by their inseparability. In other words as an event organizer you are reliant on your staff, performers and athletes to meet the needs of audience. But you have far less quality control than you would have over tangible goods (such as soft drink).

In summery the three features of services marketing are the following:

- Intangibility may include fun, entertainment, information, etc.

- Inseparability means product and provider are inseparable.
- Variability means different levels of service provided by different ushers or different responses from two or more customers to the same experiences.

Another important consideration for the event marketer is to keep in mind that an event, whether it is a one-time or annual, is highly perishable. Unsold ticket can not be put out on a rack to be sold at a reduced price or kept in store for use in the next event. Than again, an event is also different from a general store or a restaurant. A restaurant can rely on a level of passing trade. If a customer decides not to go a restaurant or general store, the restaurant owner or shopkeeper may see the customer at a latter date. But this is not the case with an event as the decision to attend or not to attend is generally made shortly before the event and is irrevocable. If a customer decides not to attend, revenue to the event organizer is completely lost.

SERVICES (intangible)	GOODS (tangible)
conference planning	room set-up
conference support services	food quality and presentation
CONFERENCE	
information, advice and problem solving	temperature, lighting
general ambience	audio-visual systems

Goods and Services Components of a Conference (Product)

Services provided at events, then, are intangible, inseparable, variable, and perishable, presenting a number of marketing challenges, since value for money is generally an issue for the consumer.

Process of Event Marketing

The event marketing process is summarized below. Ultimately the aims are to enhance the profile of the event (and associated sponsors), to meet the needs of the event audience, and, in most cases, to

establish the features of the product
identify customers (segmentation)
plan to meet audience needs
analyze consumer decision making processes
establish price and ticket programme
promote the event
evaluate marketing efforts
generate revenue.

Establish the Feature of the Product

Each event offers a range of benefits to the event audience. Some of them may include one or more of the following:

- a learning experience
- entertainment
- an opportunity to meet others
- a chance to purchase items
- a chance to see some thing unique

Generally, people attending an event want to see the product as a package of benefits. Therefore, while marketing an event an alignment between the product benefits and the needs of the audience is necessary. It may guide the design of the event and the promotional efforts. The entertainment programmes adds as value to the main benefit offered by a sporting event product.

Identify Customer

It is absolutely necessary to analyze the different motivations of the event audience and to develop a profile for each of these groups. Market segmentation is the process of analyzing the customer in groups.

Meet Audience Needs

Once customer grouping is identified, it is necessary to ensure that all three needs are met. The needs of all segments of customers are to be taken care of and none can be ignored. For example, in a music concert, generation of older music enthusiasts will be looking for a certain type of entertainment, but younger group (aged 10 to 14) needs to be entertained so that they can also gain some thing from the experience. However, many others would come for just the firework at the end. But all audiences need food and facilities. But for a particular event audience, food and beverage may not be a high priority. For some music is the priority for others it is the hype of the event and for some it is food that is important.

Analyze Consumer Decision Making

The next step is to analyze the customer's decision-making process. Research conducted in this area and information received there from is very useful in guiding promotional efforts.

Establish Price and Ticket Programme

The economic environment and the paying capacity of the audience would also need to be scanned in order to understand factors that may have an impact on discretionary spending on tickets, travel and accommodation. A comparison is required and need to be considered with other forms of entertainment available to the audience within his disposable income.

Now it is necessary to consider that the event attendance could be tied to some tourist travel to a destination. In this case, it would involve negotiations with a travel agency, extending the time laying for planning. Plans would need to be finalized long before the event, with price determined, brochures printed and advertising done. In case of an overseas event, like FIFA Football World Cup, 2010, held in South Africa, this package tour might also include air fare, accommodations and match tickets.

Finally, the desire to attend an event needs to be translated into a purchase action. If it is perceived that getting tickets is going to be difficult, some consumers might not make efforts. In fact, advance ticket selling means a better opportunity to plan for an event as well as a substantial boost to the cash flow. Any restriction on advance tickets means that the decision to attend would generally be made on the day of event and is considered impulsive.

Promotion of Event

Potential customers may have positive responses to some aspects of event and negative responses to others such as the distance to be traveled, crowding and the risk of bad weather. Customer can be divided into decision makers, follow up, influencers and purchasers.

Organizers must demonstrate the difference between an event, whether it is a concert, festival, street fair or charity fun run, from other related options. The consumer needs to know why this event is special.

Effectives Communication: The combination of text and images requires a lot of creative effort. The messages used to promote an event and the selection of an appropriate channel (both print and electronic media) are extremely important for an effective communication. These communication messages need to be disseminated among the consumers subject to time and sufficient budget available. The forms of promotional communication include brochures; posters; banners; press releases; newspapers; radio and television advertising; Internet; etc. Balloons and crowd pleasure are eye-catching promotional strategy to be used by an event organizer.

Time Available for Decision-making

This issue is; when does the consumer make the decision to attend the event? If the decision will be made two/three months before the event, marketing initiatives will be put in place at that time. If the decision will be made the weak or the day before the event, this timing of the initiative will have great implications on how, when and with what amount the advertising will be made.

CORE-MARKETING CONCEPT

- Value, Satisfaction and Quality;
- Needs, Wants and Demands;
- Product and Services;
- Exchange, Transaction and Relationships; and
- Markets.

The most important concept which event-marketing professional must know, is the societal marketing concept. As per the concept of societal marketing business organizations should determine the needs, wants and interest of target markets. After understanding the needs, wants and interest of the target market, the organization should try to deliver ultimate value to customers in a way that maintains the well being of the customers and the society. The societal marketing concept intends to safeguard the interest of the mankind and society at large.

Marketing operates within a dynamic global environment. Globalization has always been one of the most inspiring concepts, which brings changes in the concept of marketing.

SOCIETAL MARKETING CONCEPT

- Society (human welfare);
- Consumers;
- Company; and
- Societal Marketing Concept.

The societal marketing concept desires marketing to balance three considerations;

1. Immediate company profit;
2. Consumer needs and satisfaction; and
3. Society's interests;

The societal marketing concept, by balancing all the three, helps companies in achieving substantial sales and profit gains.

Marketing impact has affected individual client welfare adversely due to high prices, deceptive prices and poor after-sales service to disadvantaged consumers. It has affected the society adversely due to cultural pollution, shortage of social goods and creation of artificial scarcity and false wants. It is also impacting adversely and harming competitors by creating barriers to entry and unfair competitive practices.

Social Responsibility is what we all need for the welfare of the mankind, event manager and event experts have a major role to perform. They have to work as the expert on events and have to perform their duties in the most appropriate manner within the freedom of expression to fulfill the need of the client as well as that of the society at large. In the process they also play a key role in fuelling the engines of economic prosperity by connecting business with consumers in a mutual interchange of market information. Event planners have a lot to do, they get lots of opportunities to fall into the hands of the client and organize something acceptable to society.

Event planners are prone to the risk because of complexities in the profession, which they have opted. Adjustment with the society, amongst the family members and adjustment between the employer and the employee, all get disturbed by the tactics, which have an impact on the society at large.

MARKETING MIX

In the final analysis, the marketing efforts need to be analyzed in terms of marketing mix. The event position well, priced well, promoted effectively and distributed efficiently and all the factors must be mixed and work together for a successful outcome.

The Marketing Mix- At a Glance

Product/Service	**Place**
event venue	ticket sellers
quality of food	tour wholesalers

quality of entertainment	tourist information offices
cleanliness of venue	venue

MARKETING MIX

Price	**Promotion**
cost of ticket	advertising
cost of travel	public relations
time taken to travel	sales promotion

Price: Pricing for an entertainment event is very important. It is guided by the size of the potential audience and the selected venue. If the ticket price is too high and the paying capacity of the audience does not match with the cost of the ticket, the result will be in the half empty venue and a losing financial outcome. Simultaneously, the popularity of artist must match with the expectation of audience and the cost of the ticket. Pricing of food and beverage items is also an important consideration for customer. Any excessive cost on this count may annoy the audience.

Promotion: Promotional activities need to be chosen carefully and should be timely. Promotional advertising on radio and television are generally expensive. The most cost effective methods of promotion are feature articles in local newspaper and banners. Events could be promoted by tourism bodies and by tourism information offices at minimal costs. Internet is also being used, of late as a source of information by the event audience.

Distribution of tickets can be done through ticket sellers or at the venue, as a part of package tours. In many cases, the event product is distributed and consumed at the venue. The effectiveness of the channels should be judged on the basis of its reach to the target audience based on the circulation of the newspaper and visibility and audibility of television and radio respectively.

EVALUATION OF MARKETING EFFORTS

Evaluation needs to be done systematically by asking question such as "Where did you find out about the event ?" or "When did you decide to attend the event ?"

There are three stages at which research can be conducted: (I) Prior to the event (II) During the event and (III) After the event. The research can be both qualitative and quantitative. In the case of former it could be case studies and in case of the latter, the research generates statistics such as customers' expenditure at the event

SUGGESTED QUESTIONS

1. Define marketing. How does marketing involve the study of brand character and the creation of an event strategy?
2. What does essentially include in event marketing?
3. Draw a chart of event marketing process.
4. How would one divide the different aspects of an event into a negative and positive response of potential customer?
5. What are prime considerations of the societal marketing concept?
6. What is the importance of the evaluation of marketing efforts?

6

Event Promotion

As a part of marketing strategy, event promotion involves communicating the image and content of the event program to the potential audience. The aim of promotional strategy is to ensure that the consumer makes a decision to purchase and follows up with the actually making the purchase. The biggest obstacle and challenge of a promotional campaign is to turn intention into action. Promotion of the event is a crucial part of marketing of any event.

Elements in Promotion

- Image/Branding
- Advertising
- Publicity
- Public Relations

Image Building, Logo and Branding

The first promotional stake for any event is the development of a logo, and image for the event. This includes the color scheme and graphics to be printed on all event materials from registration forms to tickets and other merchandise. Image and logo are closely interlinked and need to be finalized well in advance. Together they are referred to as "Branding." In order to avoid any conflict over the use of color or the size of logos, it is essential to obtain the approval of sponsors involved.

The design must meet the needs of all stakeholders. It should be appealing to the audience, especially for merchandise such as T-shirts and hats. There should be a consistency in the theme and color scheme for all promotional materials. The color scheme could also be carried to the decor, fencing, flags, table-settings, banners and poster setting.

ADVERTISING

Advertising is the most important element of promotional strategy. Advertising is routed through different media of communication. Some of them are:

- Print
- Radio
- Television
- Internet
- Brochures
- Folders
- Hoardings/Billboards

For a marketing planner it is necessary to identify the reach of marketing areas and the people leaving in the market area. This should be followed by identifying the media which would be likely to reach the targeted customers. After selecting the appropriate media, keeping in mind the cost and budget provided for the event, there is a need to decide the time of the release of the advertisement. Whether it will be released a month before, a week before or a day before the event, will be guided by the nature of the event, its proximity to the targeted audience and the location of the event. These are all crucial decisions and need to be taken after taking into account different factors in a balanced way.

While preparing an advertising budget, the event planner should be fully aware of the cost of different time slots on radio and television, as well as the rates of the advertisement on different pages of newspaper and magazine. In case one wants to attract international audiences, one will need to identify the potential overseas audiences and develop a tourist package comprising of airfare, accommodation, tickets for the event and other allied facilities. Partnership arrangements can often be reached with travel agencies, airlines, and hotels, as well as with state and national tourism boards that have agreed to support and promote the event.

The content of advertisements must be informative, and of importance. It must inspire decision making and action to attend or purchase. Let's look at the following advertisement by an event company for its wedding rental products and services:

'We provide six-arm gold candelabra in the Victorian style, silk flowers, tweed lights, fairy lights, table overlays (in organza, jacquard and cotton), chair covers with sashes and ceiling drapes. We set up for you.'

In this advertisement there is a lot of information but absolutely no inspiration. A number of descriptive adjectives would certainly have enhanced the text, as well as the possibility of customers' buying their services!

In contrast, the following advertisement for an unusual event is much more creative. It would be very difficult to attract an event audience if only the facts of a blood donation were presented and if the promotional team has realized this by making this event into something not to be missed.

WE WANT YOUR BLOOD!

Millard Clinic Blood Drive Week

August 10-15 with the grand finale (don't miss this) on August 15 (10 a.m. to 9 p.m.) Greendale Clinic's last drive was a huge success. This year our target is 3,000 units of blood. Sponsors have donated ten major prizes as well as minor prize for all other donors. Our top prize, a trip for two to Hawaii, will be presented at the grand finale. We will have a health advice booth, a complimentary espresso kiosk, food booths, a craft fair, afternoon. Attendance is free and all donors will receive a sponsor prize, and will be entered into the drawing for the major prizes. Parking is available on Grant St.

Advertising brings excitement to an otherwise boring event.

The advertising message needs to meet the motivational needs of the audience at the same time that it assists the decision-making process by supplying the necessary facts.

PUBLICITY

The distinction between the advertising and the publicity is that, advertising is paid, where as publicity is free. Free publicity for an event can be secured by running a careful publicity campaign with the media. This involves developing and disseminating press releases to journalists and then following it up and collecting the feedback, sometimes interviews by journalists of the chief of the organizers will also be necessary. For a successful publicity, the organizer of the event needs to be fully conversant with the functioning of the media, its various functionaries, both in print and electronic media. For example, in print media it is the editor or the news editor who could be contacted. For the news item, feature writer for any feature or article, who can be also contacted. Similarly in the broadcast media, it is the station manager or the news reader in radio who could be contacted for the same. For television it is the programme producer or the station director who can be contacted. In any case, or in any media, the news worthiness of the event is required to be explained fully and satisfactorily to the concerned executive.

The aim of the press release is to stimulate media interest in the event and achieve positive and cost-effective publicity. Many event organizers post their press releases on their web pages. A launch for mega event is generally held much prior to the event to which the media and celebrities are invited for shows. The press release is also distributed on these occasions. For the success of the occasion it is essential that the launch function be well attended and media should report the event in a positive manner. In cases of smaller events, a press release may be sent to the local papers and local radio station and it may serve the purpose. Since the staff working on smaller local papers are extremely busy, they may be provided with a ready-to-print article along with photographs, logos and quotations whatever possible.

Though there are no fixed guidelines for preparing a press release, if the following steps are taken for the same, the readers may take notice of the news about the event:

- There must be something to appeal to the reader in the first two sentences, which is called 'intro' in journalistic parlance. This may motivate the readers to go through the entire news item about the event mentioned in the press release.
- All the facts must be covered and any what, when where, why and how, arising in the mind of reader must be dully answered in the press releases. The reader wants to know what is to happen, when it is to happen why it is to happen where it is to happen and how the event will be performed and will be resolved. The reader would also want to know how the things will be resolved in any crisis, if so arising could be controlled. If the press release is promoting an event, all information such as the venue, date, time and other related information about the event should be included in it.
- The press release should be short and to the point.
- Layout is extremely important.
- Contact details should be provided.
- Photographs should be captioned.
- Quotes from senior staff and sponsors and other stakeholders may be included.
- It should also describe all possible benefits for the audience from the event.
- All necessary information for booking and registering should also be included.

Apart from free media publicity, official tourism organizations may also provide tourist information to visitors through their offices or Websites. Brochures distributed to such offices can provide valuable information to the potential event audience. The purpose is to ensure that the event is listed as wide as possible.

PUBLIC RELATIONS

The role of public relations is to manage and improve the images of the organization and the images of the event in the minds of the audience and targeted public. This is achieved mainly through press releases. The up-to-date information through the press release along with photographs, provide the media with the background material, they need to develop the story about the event. Media briefing can also be arranged before and during the event. High profile people such as celebrities, entertainers or athletes can also be associated in media briefing if they can enhance the publicity of the event.

Another important role of public relations is to inform and clarify the media, if there is any negative incident of any kind. For this, an incident-reporting system needs to be in place so that chief of the event management team is fully informed, and enable them to brief the media as and when required. It is also necessary to issue a press release or appear in an interview with the media persons, if any such incident occurs. This role of public relations can be highly sensitive one, and PR personnel should be in a position to handle the media in a professional and efficient way. He should also be fully conversant about the causes of the incident if any. Another positive role of public relations is the entertainment of the guests and VIPs attending the event. Normally PR personnel would need to follow the following guidelines:

- Attentive to the needs and expectations of the guests of the event;
- Fully aware of their cultural expectations and flexible in responses to their behavior;
- Informative and helpful as a host;
- Proactive to meet the required protocol; and
- Able to converse with the guests easily.

It is particularly necessary to know the details, such as official titles, correct names, and correct pronunciation of the name etc of the foreign guests of the event or guests of event sponsors. As an event manager or the organizer you need to know the reasons why your company is hosting these guests. It may be business objectives, such as sponsor product awareness or negotiation in organizing the functions. Research is, therefore, essential to determine how to meet the needs of the guests and the expectation of the sponsored. According to Roger Axtell (1990), the effective multicultural host has the following attributes:

- Being respectful
- Tolerating ambiguity
- Relating well to people
- Being nonjudgmental
- Personalizing one's observations (not making global assertions about people or places)
- Showing empathy
- Being patient and persistent

As seen from the preceding, there are a number of roles for the public relations manager, or indeed for all members of the event team. The opportunity to sell an event occurs every time the telephone is answered or an inquiry is made by a potential customer. Because customer relations becomes the role of everyone involved in an event. Training in this area is recommended and necessary it should focus on the event information likely to be required by the customer. Training ties with the planning process and the distribution of information to all concerned from beginning to the end.

An event manager might also become involved in public relations functions in certain situations like:

- Making travel arrangement;
- Meeting and greeting at the airport;
- Providing transportations;
- Entertaining at event and meals;
- Organizing meetings;
- Providing tours details;

While conducting a small group around the venue, some other actions can also be taken:

- Plan the tour allowing enough time to see every thing;
- Advise and inform the guests about your plan;
- Ensure time for a break and refreshment;
- Make available maps to the people to get their bearings;
- Pause frequently allowing the guests to ask questions and be graceful in replying;
- Make sure that every one can see and hear you, treat every one in equals;
- Be patient as speak positively at an appropriate volume;
- Be flexible in the tour keeping in mind the convenience of guests;

In promoting an event, analyze and understand the needs of the target market. It is also necessary to keep in mind that the person purchasing the product may not the consumer, it may be the parent. In this case the promotional efforts need to assist with decision-making processes within the family. Likewise, a sponsor may be making a substantial investment in the event and may have high expectations of the event, which may or may not be consistent with those of the event audience.

Summary

The task of promoting an event to the audience in the optimal way and at the most beneficial time is the first and foremost requirement. The second is to meet the needs of all stakeholders and to maximize public relations benefits to the customers at all levels.

ROLE OF MEDIA IN EVENT PROMOTION

Events, exhibitions, trade fairs, conferences are all part of the community relation policy of an organizations. Organizations may plan their community relations programmes according to an agreed policy. Organizations can act consistently in making decisions about what it wants to support and community has a clear idea of their chances of success in applying for support. The responsibility for community relation policy may lie with the public relations department or elsewhere in the organization but usually the top management takes a decision. As a part of the promotion policy of an organization, members of the local community might be given free training by the organization.

Publicity professional has to communicate decision makers the specific role their discipline plays, that differentiates it from paid publicity. In paid publicity one can choose his message and medium of communication. But in a paid message public sometimes have skepticism. Readers and viewers look for and take more credible the news item than the paid publicity advertisements. Public Relations experts use different publicity media which fall broadly in two categories; print media and Electronic media. The print media include daily weekly, fortnightly, monthly, quarterly, half yearly and annual newspapers and magazines. Some of the magazines are published for the general public, some for women, some professionals, scientific and ethnic as well as special interest groups. Electronic media include Radio and television. Newspapers publish features articles, etc along with news.

Print Media

Print media is essential for pre-event, mid-event and post event publicity by covering the event as in the report of the success of the event. Print media enjoy more confidence of the readers, influence public opinion, appear regularly and cover local and regional areas intensively. Newspapers also cover the special interests of women, business communities, sports enthusiast, communication experts, researcher and a number of others through features, marketing stories, human interest stories and others also. Usually events get publicity due to the efforts of communication professionals, public relations experts and due to the brand image of event sponsor. Pre-event publicity is used to spread information about the exact details of event such as venue, date and time of the event and also to distribute entry forms, feedback schedules, discount coupon etc, the mid-event publicity is generated by presenting celebrities, performers or sportspersons before the media representatives. The post-event coverage is generated through public relations efforts by distributing press release with photographs of the event and comments of the experts about the event to different media for coverage. But the event organizer has little control over the post event coverage. The post event coverage is the task in which journalists see that a balanced story appears in the paper which has both positive and negative reflection in a broader sense.

Magazines are appropriate media for product publicity, feature stories and pictorial publicity. They can be read leisurely and thoroughly. Any special issue will not only be read by many but would also be preserved for future reference. Magazines, which could provide space to tell a complete unbiased story, are particularly suitable for service and educational publicity articles. The quality of paper and lovable color combination of magazines make them ideal for picture publicity. Print media offers special supplements related to the event just at the time of the sprit of the event is being felt by the common man. Events like Valentine day, Onom, Baisakhi, Holi, Diwali, Chrismas day and events like sports tournaments, exhibitions and trade fairs get maximum coverage in the print media. Such event specific issues are considered helpful in providing publicity and coverage to these events. Also the increased advertisement in the print media increased the economy of the media unit. Special rates for advertising are charged for insertions in such special issues. Even at the time of such events as in the festive season, audiences look forward to such issues for more information and more focused insight into the events.

ELECTRONIC MEDIA

Electronic media comprise of radio and television. Radio and television have an all-reaching capacity as media of communication.

Radio is still considered as a mass media which is available at all destinations, irrespective of the distance or physical connectivity with different parts of the country. Radio is mainly used for pre-event publicity. It can also be used for post-event coverage, if planned. After the advent of FM radio, the reach of radio has become unmatchable. It does not require a power supply and can invariably found in the hands of both literates and illiterates, rickshaw pullers to taxi-drivers' to senior executives' costly cars.

Television media is considered as the most potent media, as it covers pre-event clips, mid-event and post event coverage. With the launch of satellite channels along with cable television networks, television as media of mass communication has increased the scope and coverage of publicity and advertising through these media of mass communication. Most events get both live and recorded coverage in the television media. These days cable television has reached millions of homes and the local channels of cable television usually broadcast the event held in the locality and the playing the role of television as a mass media. The live as well as recorded coverage of Navaratri, Dandiya by the various cable networks is one of the most popular media coverage during Dandiya seasons. Similarly Ganeshshostava and Durga Puja are also widely covered even by major news channels like Doordarshan, Zee TV, NDTV, Star News and a number of other TV Channels.

DISPLAY MEDIA

The display media comprises of hoardings put up at public places, neon signs which keep placing and changing wall painting and posters put up at railway stations airports and on streets. Panels attached to kiosks on lamp posts buses, railway compartments taxies. Exhibitions, trade shows and fairs, banners at retail outlets window display, sky balloons etc are another way of display media.

PARTICIPATION PLANNING IN EVENTS

Trade shows is an important medium to project material, products, services and ideas of an organizations to the public at large. The aim is to develop and increase awareness about the brand name of the company and its products to boost sales. Specialized events of the short duration, is organized in the trade fairs throughout the world, as the general trade fair has lost its significance except for consumer goods. The participation in trade shows enables an organization to display its product before a large audience. The decision to participate can be taken after ensuring that the audiences in the trade shows are those that can not be reached effectively through other promotional activities. It is assumed that public relations, publicity, advertising and sales promotion are used to promote the objective of the organization by promoting a common thing, which can give a favorable result.

While planning for participation in the trade fare, event or exhibition, make sure that which of the product is the right one to be displayed. A decision about a particular product to be shown is to be taken well in advance. Often, trade magazines publish special features in collaboration with the trade shows organizations and the magazines need photographs and other publicity materials. Research plays an important role in planning as well as promoting events. Event planners must always be aware of what special additions are coming up and with what deadline schedules. Promoters should think of the new model that is being displayed. Trade shows exhibition should reveal innovation and newness.

Every event planner and event organizer should give preference to local promotional efforts. Mere participation in a trade fair or exhibition can not provide desired results as expected by the organizers. It is necessary to evaluate whether the whole exercise was performed as planned and its amounts of success in achieving the desired results.

Event planning being the most important task in organizing the event, exhibitions, trade as well as fairs, need thorough research and careful understanding of the need and desire of the client. The client might request something that could be impossible to provide but it is essential for event planner to provide the client something that could benefit the client in the budget approved for the purpose of organizing an event or exhibition. While working as a public relations expert in any corporate organization the expert should thoroughly go through the proposals before short-listing any event planner to give a presentation on the event proposal. Scrutiny of most efficient event planning agency is not the only task which is usually handled by the communication expert but the task which is usually handled by the communication experts. In addition, it is the responsibility of the public relations professional to suggest the most appropriate course of action on the part of the organization also to suggest about the type of media coverage, promotional strategy, booking of venue and about other aspects related to the event planning

EVENT CHARGES

The event charges are required to be fixed keeping in view the economic and social standards of clients as well as employees. Failing which one is likely to face challenges which might have never expected. In all business or profession the objective is to make a sale, which would result in the betterment of the organization. An event organization depends on the clients for home it works. After all it gets payment from them in exchange the services as expert rendered to them. The common aim of both the event management organization and the client is to earn and grow. No event management organization can charge wishfully from the client in exchange of the services rendered by it. While charging the client any fee for the services rendered to the company, one has to justify its demand. Every good effort on its part, helps an organization to achieve the purpose of developing good relation with both internal and external public.

While quoting any cost to the client, each organization evaluates the bases on which it wants to charge an amount from its client. There should be an understanding, image management and confidence which are based on experience and knowledge. The objective in the event management industry is not merely to promote the organization, but to develop the business and offer expert services to as many clients as possible. A strategic thinking based on an overall assessment of various factor are the guiding principle of the decision making in how an organization is going to charge from its clients. There are pros and cons to the various methods, but they all serve a purpose in tailing an organization about whom it will be doing business with, for the planners. Though the client and the event planner are different entities, both have the same goal and objectives to stage a successful event. Any promotional campaign must at the first instance clearly set out its objectives. It must also decide the areas to be covered and the people or the section of the community to be reached.

Success of an event brings the client further closer to the goal the organization intended to achieve, where as for the event planner success means that they are running a profitable business. Both the client and the event planner want the event to be successful as both of them want to get maximum benefit from the event. For the event charges, a balance between payment for expertise and getting an economical deal is required.

Both the parties have commercial and individual identity angles. The planner seeks to maximize profits and client seeks to keep the cost to the minimum. Sometimes striking a deal which safeguards interest of both parties may be difficult as well as manipulative. The fee system in the event industry is similar to that of in advertising industry. An advertising agency receives a fifteen per cent straight commission from the media for advertisement placed by the agency. The service charges system is some what similar for the charges from the clients in the event planning business.

While quoting the amount to be charged the event planner usually follows the following four different ways. These are:

(I) Percentage of the Total Event Cost;

(II) Flat Fee;

(III) Package Price;
(IV) Hourly Rate

Percentage of the Total Event Cost

The traditional fifteen percent commission remains a form of agency income especially for modestly budgeted accounts. Clients and agency may agree to a relationship in which the rate is fixed at less than fifteen percent. This generally applies to large budget accounts, the larger the budget, the lower the rate for the agency. Event planning companies do not always charge the same percentage for each type of event they do or to every client. The percentage charge may vary as it is based on different factors. The type of event has an impact on the percentage charged because different types of projects require different level of expertise and can involve the additional expenses of key people such as creative directors, producers, art designers, writers that may not normally be required. So it should be clearly understood by the event planner as well as client that just by the nature of their design and the elements that are included, event might be much more labor intensive or demand special attention.

So event planning agencies come up with "creative costing" methods that can provide them additional revenue, such as listing the hotel rate so that it appears to be when they are receiving the commission being paid either directly to them or sub-contracted from their payment to the hotel. Planners need to provide value for money and clients to be willing to pay for professional help. Event planners charge the amount which they think is justified for the services they would be providing to the clients, where as the client who hires the event companies wants to nickel and dying their suppliers and those involved in the planning process are short listed. They also change suppliers very often in search of the best deal, not the quality service. Contracting the cheapest service provider may not prove the least expensive at the end of the day.

But both the client and event planners must think that they can not compromise on the standard of event planning and coordination. In case of event charges based on the percentage of the total event costs, it is necessary to clearly define exactly what cost will be covered under the banner. All programme elements are listed and then percentage charges are applied. What is included and what not included in the event charges needs to be clearly mentioned in the contract papers.

If the event planners and the clients are looking to build long-term relationship, they can offer a preferred percentage rate on their actual event charges, to selected clients. This is usually done in case of signing a long term contract say for three to five years for some specific business or conference or all of their business and social event planning needs, during the period. When the client received a preferred fee rate both the client and the planner are making a contracted commitment to do business together on long term basis. Both parties involved recognize the benefits equally.

Some clients need more handholding, more personal involvement and contact. Other clients require multiple meetings that continuously pull staff away from the task at hand which is not favorable for the event planner as well as the client in long-term. In such cases time consumed must be compensated, if it is above and beyond what is deemed reasonable.

Flat Fee

Some clients and the planners may consider opting for a flat fee against the one based on percentage. Event charges based on percentage can exceed a fair rate of return if the budget is in the upper limits. Some events can be intricate and take thousands of man-hour to coordinate and produce, but other may just sound as complicated to someone who is uninformed. Clients unfamiliar with what is required to produce, a custom audio- visual presentation, for example could easily end up in excessive amounts in fees if they are not dealing with a reputed event planner.

Every event is organized with mutual agreement between the event planner and the client, both the parties are required to maintain the quality of the event. At times in the process of event planning, decision makers make some changes, budgets are increased, items are taken out or added in a variety of things and when the costing is redone, the issue of rates may come under scrutiny. Clients preferred the flat rate to get the maximum from the event planner by paying the flat fee. Event planners prefer to offer the flat fee to client with big budget and big brand name, in hope to not work hard for getting media coverage.

Package Price

Event planners may also offer a package price. One method is to simple list all inclusive in one price that also includes the management fees. The inclusions are detailed but the individual pricing is not broken down. Taxes and service charges are often listed separately, but this is only to allow the planner to advertise a visually attractive price to consumers. In package price, each change involves a complete new costing for every alternation. Before entering into any agreement, the event planner and the client should agree to the terms and conditions and the plan of action for the event before. Only after this the event planner should start working on the plan.

Hourly Rate

For an event planning agency it is impossible to offer services on hourly basis. Freelancers commonly charge an hourly rate rather than a set fee. Freelancers are generally sub-contracted by public relations agencies to assist them in event planning and operations. Corporations may also hire them for special in-house projects. The rate and payment schedule is negotiated up-front, the total number of hours to be used to complete the task, remains the unknown factor.

A planner may be brought in on consultancy basis, when a company such as an advertising or public relations agency receives a request to plan a large scale event for one of their clients. A planner may be contracted to act as a consultant under the public relations agency or an event management agency. Consultants are responsible for drafting event strategies and communication strategies in coordination with other experts involved in the process of event planning. Expert advice is considered to be helpful at all stages of event planning. If the event works go well certain event companies may also like to enter into contract with consultants for future events they may organize for the present and in future as well. In addition to the hourly rates charged by free lancer, other expenses could include mileage and parking, if required to commute the official site of the event. However these items need to be agreed upon and mentioned clearly in the contract papers.

SUGGESTED QUESTIONS

1. What are the function and its importance of event promotion in marketing strategy?
2. What are the important elements of event promotion?
3. What roles do logo and branding play in event promotion?
4. Define the following:
   (a) Image/Branding
   (b) Advertising
   (c) Publicity, and
   (d) Public Relation.
5. How are event charges fixed?
6. Write shorts notes on:
   (a) Percentage of total event cost,
   (b) Flat fee,
   (c) Package price, and
   (d) Hourly rate

7

Event Conceptualization, Document Design and Planning

Event Conceptualization

The event conceptualization is the creative element that inspires many to embark on careers in event management. Although it is absolutely necessary to be creative inspired, innovative ideas must also be reasonably practical under the limitation of the cost, venue and safety of event. The other limitation on creativity is the taste of the client. Simultaneously, both the event organizer and the client have a clear idea of the purpose of the event.

The event conceptualization is impacted by certain elements of an event. There are a number of elements that need to be considered in event conceptualization they include the purpose of the event, the theme of the event, the venue of the event, the audience of the event, the timing of the event and the financial limitation for the event.

Purpose of the Event

The purpose of event will be the main driving factor in event conceptualizations and its planning. The focus of the purposes of the event is generally information and entertainment. The main purpose of organizing an event is making a profit, for others it may be to improve the positioning of its Brand name. In some cases it may be community purposes. The organizing of festivals is an example of an event with a community purpose.

Theme of the Event

The theme of the event should be linked to the purpose of the event. It should also be compatible with the needs of guests and consistent in all respects. For example, a color scheme adopted by an event should be repeated on all items prepared for the event such as tickets, uniforms, décor, posters and merchandise. This technique helps attendees to identify with the theme.

When coming up with ideas for a theme it is important to consider the range of suitable venues available, keeping in mind budget limitations and other considerations.

Venue of the Event

The options for an event manager in choosing an event venue are categorized as; standard venue and an unusual venue. An unusual venue requires decorations, like lighting, sound and catering, and also pose challenges in unusual settings. There are many more factors that need to be taken into account in selecting an event venue. But the over all strategy remains to aim for the best possible suiting to the needs of client and the audience, and at the lowest possible cost.

Event Audience

The needs of all participants must be considered before conceptualizing an event and giving final touches to the concept. Of course, audiences are varied and each audience is different and the event manager needs to go with the flow and to direct the event to meet audience response. This method can also involve some changes in the plan.

Financial Considerations

The financial consideration is important at the early stage of event conceptualization and design. Initial financial estimates can get out of control and the choice of event concept can certainly contribute to this problems. As it is happening in the case of the Commonwealth Games, 2010 (Delhi) for which, the estimated cost in 2003 of Rs 655 crore has increased to Rs 11,494 crore, in 2010 which is 17.5 times more than the estimated cost. Also it is possible that good ideas could be knocked on the head at an early stage if they do not appear financially viable. It is possible to come up with concepts that are startling in their simplicity and that are also cost effective. This is where the creative and rational aspects of the event manager's abilities can come into conflict. Some times the creative aspects win at the expense of the companies profit on the event. For example, the Government of India is pouring unlimited amount to make the Commonwealth Games 2010, a grand success for the sake of the national prestige.

Timing of the Event

The timing of the event is often linked to the season or weather. The Commonwealth Games 2010, is being organized in the month of October, after the rainy season will be over. The broadcasting of the event to international audiences is another consideration. The evaluation of an event concept takes into consideration, the time-related factor such as season and duration. Generally the weather does affect an event. The event planners take into considerations the time of year, normal weather patterns and already scheduled events. As the hot summer during the summer season and heavy rains could have adversely affected the Games, the Commonwealth Games 2010 have been organized in Delhi, after both summer and rainy seasons are over.

Skills for Preparing an Event Proposal

The earlier mentioned points are necessary to be considered in an event concept. But it is the event expert who synchronizes all these elements to make them homogenous and put up as a proposal before the event organizer. Event experts must know how to write as per the guidelines of public relations writers integrating communication tools. But the command over language is certainly going to benefit the event management expert. Few people are born writers. Like any other discipline quality writing requires hard work, dedications, and patience. The more one writes, the better he should become, provided he has acquired the basics. Writing basics do not change significantly from one form to another. Words have the power to present a food as a most intelligent geek.

Event expert must have the power of words in his command for the over-development of the image of his organization. The basis of writing must be clear to the event expert. The capability to think and act suits the concepts of writing to perform well and the writer must think before writing. Few people can observe an event, grasp its meaning immediately and sit down to compose several paragraphs. The essence of an event writing is that what ever information, ideas or emotion the writer wants to communicate to readers must be communicated in an unambiguous and organized way.

The event planners must have the basics clear and know how to develop a fresh event concept document. The term document describes any thing one might write in the language. Well designed documents such as event concept, manuals, and reports have been important in the business world where writers have to compete for the attention of the readers. The more people understand what you are trying to say, the better you can stimulate action. The simple writing is the better writing clarity is essential in writing, that is, each word, each sentence and each paragraph must be the keys to clarifying the tightness.

Designing of Document

Document design is becoming increasingly important. The information explosion has placed unprecedented demands on instructors and students' time, so professional articles and student essays must be accessible as possible. Facilitating today's computers and printers provide academic writers and event document designers with design strategies that were once prohibitively expensive.

Good document design promotes readability but this depends on the purpose and the audience and other elements of one's writing situation such as the subject of the writing. The writer must have the target audience in mind and tailor the message to communicate to them, to win the minds of specific audience, the writer must be willing to sacrifice certain other thinks.

The paragraphing and clean topic sentences to guide readers should be used by the writer. In more complex documents such as research papers, event proposal and business report, headings help readers to read at a glance the organization of a document, as it provides some visual cue for readers. Headings serve a number of other functions depending on the needs of different readers. Headings will help to find it quickly to readers when they are looking for information. Headings should be brief and informative.

While writing event proposal plans and event evaluation report, consistency should be maintained in the style. For writing a good document, the topic of the document, expectations of the readers from the document, the identity of the readers, the level of the understanding of the readers should be kept in mind.

The event management experts must learn the basics of writing and try to write as per the need of the hour. The writing in simple layman's language might benefit the readers. Client is always short of time and the use of big words and a lengthy letter or proposal may not yield desired results. A simple writing can give more desire result and success.

Designing the Event

The creativity and creative process are essentially linked to the purpose of the event. The main creative elements that are to be considered in designing an event are:

Theme, Layout, Décor, Suppliers, Technical, Requirements, Entertainment, Catering and other Logistics of the Concepts

The theme of the event should ideally appeal to all senses tactile, smell, taste, visual and auditory (Gold blatt). The lay out should provide comforts to the audience to fill in the venue to create a positive ambience. The options for fabrics, decorative items stage props drapes and table setting, all to be rented, should be investigated before deciding on the event theme. Good relationship with suppliers of all commodities will ensure the supply of quality products, including, fresh flower and best produce that the market can supply. Technical requirement to be used need to be tested thoroughly. And technically possible event concept may be considered for staging. Entertainment is central for events and it should suit the purpose of the event. The needs of event audience are of paramount importance and must be considered carefully while making the decision. The quality of foods and prompt services are the consideration while making a decision about catering. Creative event planning frequently requires unique or unusual food and beverage products that can be time consuming to find.

While considering an event concept, a careful balance is required between the creative and rational aspects of decision making. Brain storming among the members of planning team may generate ideas and these need to be considered as to their feasibility.

Event designers are required to undertake the following task for making an event successful one:

- Creative Concept Development
- Venue Selection
- Permits and Access
- Hiring of Equipment
- Lighting and Sound Requirements
- Entertainment Requirements
- Menu Requirements

Analysis and Evaluation of the Concept

There are certain problems and pitfalls that can occur if they are not considered at an early stage of the conceptualization of the event. They can put a negative impact on the creativity of the event managers. Prier to involvement in any event conceptualization, it is necessary to conduct an analysis of your competitors. The compatibility of the proposal with the laws and regulation is to be ensured in the creativity and the staging of events. The consideration of the marketing of the event is very important part of the initial concept and planning. Another major consideration for an event at the planning stage is to assess its community impact. It is essential for the event organizer to explain the community benefit and other impacts are to be considered in the event proposal. Measures to counteract the impact of weather are essential aspects of event feasibility planning. Finally, the event concept needs a very careful analysis of the investment and revenue to be generated from the propose event

PLANNING

Planning can be described as "the process through which we determine how best to commit present available resources in order to influence future events. A proper attention given to planning before starting any business, trade or any activity leads to a sound decision making.

Planning is a must for achieving success in any event management. The importance of planning is never ignored either in event industry or any other industry. Planning has now become specialized, and is being applied to more and more aspects of our business and personal lives. It is being recognized as a task essential to event management.

Planning can be used by the event planner to meet all internal and external objectives of his client. Every element becomes an opportunity to bring the event planner closer to the goal. Every aspect of event planning is very important. In the process of event planning the event planner must know as much as possible about the objectives of the organizations, behind the event. Planning is the key to success and before undertaking the job, the event planner should foresee what kind of facility might be required to provide and be aware of the action to be taken in providing the most professional service. While formulating a plan it has two purposes; one to provide an extraordinary event to the client, fulfilling the needs of the client and also to generate predictable response before the actual event takes place.

Event planning is one of the most important ingredient in the process of event management. A proposal meeting between the event planner team and client's team, enables the event planner to understand the objectives of the organizations along with event elements demographics, budget for the event and the past history of the events held, if any. Every plan needs thorough research for which meetings and discussions play an important role. Before designing any event, the event planner should have a complete knowledge of the conditions. The event planner is responsible for creating the condition in which these events take place within the limit of the budget of the client. Strategic event planner begins by reviewing the groups dynamics, which plays an important role in determining the style of the event. Though generating maximum profit is the aim of the client and every event planner also tries to fulfill those tasks by providing professional advice and services. On the other hand the sales team prefers that events have a competitive edge.

Planning Process

Planning is the process that involves the determination of any future course of action. Planning is necessary to review why we need to take an action, what type of action is best suited, how to move towards the process of taking action and what time should be needed for action to be taken. All these aspects are the process, which determines in advance the future accomplishment and the means to achieve them. For an event planner it means drawing a blue print of the activities to be undertaken for staging the event, anticipated problems etc.

Need of Planning

Planning is primarily needed for two reasons:

1. Committing and allocating an organization's available resources for achieving its stated goals, and

2. Anticipating the future problems and opportunities.

Planning is the process which determines the future course of action. It is concerned basically with the future and requires forecasting of the future situation. It is undertaken at all levels of the organization and is not restricted to a certain situation only. Planning is flexible and is based on future conditions which are always dynamic and an adjustment is needed among the various factors in planning.

Advantage of Planning

Advantages of planning are manifold:

- Things can be looked at in totality,
- Problems and challenges can be anticipated
- Better utilization of resources is possible
- Proper resources can be done
- Unproductive work and wastage can be minimized.

Types of Plans

Generally plans can be of two types: **Strategic Plans and Tactical Plans**

Strategic plans are devised to meet the goals of the organization, where as tactical plans are devised to implement strategic plans. Plans are the mission statement, which defines the goals of the organization. Strategic plans decide the aims and policy of the organization. The programmes and methods for their fulfillment are also detailed in the plan. In order to formulate a strategic plan one can begin with asking the following questions:

- What service is to be provided by you?
- What sort of competition do you have?
- What are the resources and infrastructural needs?
- What unique features you offer?
- What is the prime motive behind this event?
- What kind of target audience is expected to visit?

- What type of results you want to achieve after the event is over?
- Who all are expected to be involved in the decision-making process?
- What is the level of expertise required for event planning?
- What kinds of approvals are to be taken for creating a plan?
- What is the budget in hand?

A strategic plan enables you meet future contingencies; correct errors; take time decisions and avoid deviations. Whereas tactical planning determines the tasks to be accomplished, determines responsibility, allocates resources and sets measurements for every task. Besides these two types of plans, there are certain other types of plans dealt with by managers in their routine. These may involve individual activity, department activity or entire organizational activity. Such plans are related to policy matter, procedures, methodology quality assurance, projects or strategies:

Planning Skills

Planning requires certain skills like the ability to think ahead, forecast future trends, state organizational goals, choice of strategy and achieve performance standards, etc. Planners must be able to determine the framework of purposes, which are related to the organization's development and business success. There is a multiplicity of objectives like: **profitability, growth, social responsibility, survival, continuity,** etc.

Steps in Planning Process

Different planning processes are applicable for different organizations and different types of plans. It is because various factors of the planning process may differ from plan to plan or organization to organization. Then again, the style of working of a particular management professional or even planner is different from that of another professional or planner. Roughly, the following stages of a planning process are to be observed by any planner:

- **Perception of Opportunity:** The knowledge, of the strength and weaknesses the level of the organization, gives an understanding why the organizations wants to solve uncertainties and the vision of what is expected to be gained from the step.
- **Establishing Objectives:** The organizational and event objectives specified the results expected and indicate the end point of what is to be done, where the primary emphasis is to be placed and what is to be accomplished through various types of plans.
- **Planning Premises:** Planning premises are both internal and external. Internal factors include policies, resources of different types and ability of the organization to withstand business pressures. External premises include total factors like political, social, technology plans and actions of competitors, policies of the government etc.
- **Identification of Alternatives:** Various alternatives are identified based on organizational objectives and planning premises. The selected alternative is then reduced and the most promising ones is taken for detailed analysis. The concept of alternatives suggests that a particular objective can be achieved through actions. This is followed by evaluation of alternatives and attempt is made to evaluate how much each alternative contributes to the business objectives in the light of its resources and constraints.
- **Formulation of Supporting Plan:** Once the basic plan is formulated, various plans are derived so as to support the main plan. These derivative plans are formulated out of the main plan and they support it.
- **Establishing Sequence of Activities:** After formulating the basic and derivatives plans, the sequence of activities is determined in order to put the plans into action. Service capabilities should be analyzed in the light of the business, really in terms of end, provides a different perspective of the business.

Features of a Plan

Introduction of the Project
Market Assessment
Size of the Project
Organizational Structure
Infrastructural Requirements
Manpower Requirements
Capital Estimates and Resources
Profits
Time Schedules.

Developing a Mission/Purpose Statement

To develop the event concept involves defining the purpose and aims of the event along with the specific objectives on which the success of the event will be measured. All stakeholders are required to be provided with a good understanding of the event concept before you proceed further. If your client is the one funding the event the provision of a clearly developed concept, plan and evaluation strategy will generally avoid problems down the line.

The first step is to develop a simple statement that summarizes the purpose or the mission of the event. Some times, the purpose of the event becomes less and less clear as the event approaches. Different stakeholders have different interest and this situations can lead sometimes to a change of focus of which most stakeholders are not aware. The purpose of an event could be for example, "to commemorate the history of our town in a historically authentic parade that involves the community and is supported by the community. In contrast a sporting event may have as its mission statement, "to attract both loyal team supporters and first-time supporter in an effort to improve ticket sales and thus the viability of the competition and the venue." The mission statement should ensure that planning and implementation do not get off the track and the initial intent is realized.

Aims of the Event

The purpose of an event can be broken down further into general aims and specific measurable objectives. An event could have one or more of the following aims:

- Improving community attitudes to health and fitness
- Raising funds for a charitable cause
- Injecting funds into the local economy
- Raising awareness of a charitable or political campaign
- Increasing tourist numbers to a specific destination
- Extending the tourist season
- Raising the profile of the town or city
- Celebrating a historical event
- Launching a new product
- Increasing product sales
- Producing media coverage
- Felicitating an award winner
- Building team loyalty
- Providing entertainment.

Aims vary widely from one event to another and this is one of the challenges for the event manager. One event might have a social impact focus, whereas another might be profit-oriented. Every thing to do with the event can not reinforce the purpose and the goals. Choice of colors, entertainment, presentation and so on, much of all works together in order to fulfill the purpose and goals of event. The recognition of aim must be established early in the negotiation process and remembered during all the planning stages.

The goals of an event provide the foundation for many aspects of the planning process. An event organizer, who gets distracted from the stated goals, is likely to clash with the organizing committee and others stake holders. When working with clients it is also essential to identify the goals early and to use them to inform the planning process. Sometimes more enthusiasm for the theme or the entertainment overrides the goals and planning goes awry. If, for example, the goals were to increase consumer recognition of the main sponsor, it would be necessary to develop specific objectives and take steps to ensure that they were achieved. At the end of the event, there could be one or more measures in place to indicate the outcomes of the event. In this case the result of a survey indicating percentage levels of sponsor recognition by the event audience. As an event manager, you need to show in a measurable way, how the goals have been achieved. Developing objectives may help you to do this.

Objectives of the event

The goals are used to develop detailed and specific objectives of the event. Ideally, objectives should be realistic and measurable. Targets, percentages and sales are generally the factors used to measure objectives. For example, an objective could be "to increase the participation level in the community fun walk to 1,00,000 , including a cross-section of age groups ranging from 15 to 60 plus this target to be reached by the 2,011 event." The number of participants and the ages of participants would be the measures of this objective, where as a survey on training undertaken in preparation for the walk would indicate less tangible outcomes such as changes in exercise patterns and attitudes of the community towards fitness and health. Another example, as one objective of an event organizer might be to increase awareness of the products of a sponsor, the main objective might be to convert this awareness into sales, which would be an even more successful outcome. Surveys of spectators and television viewers are used to demonstrate changes in awareness of a sponsor's products.

For a proper evaluation, it is necessary that the aims and objectives of an event must be clear in the first place. Objectives are generally evaluated by the following measures:

- Size of audience
- Demographics of audience
- Average expenditure of audience
- Sponsor recognition levels

- Sales of sponsor products
- Economic impact of the event
- Profit

Smart objectives are specific, measurable, achievable, realistic and time related.

Event Proposal

At this stage of planning the proposal should include the purpose, the aims and the objectives of the event, along with details on organization, physical lay out and the social, environmental and economic impact, if applicable. Maps and models may also prove useful in explaining and illustrating the event concept and more detailed plans could insure the client's expectations as being realistic. An event proposal at a glance may be like this:

Event Proposal—At a Glance

Event Description

Event Name
Event Type
Event Location
Event Date
Event Duration
Event Aims and Objectives

Event Planning Tools

Event planning tools include organizations chart, maps, models, Gantt charts, run sheets and check lists. These tools are very useful for presenting material and information to clients, members of staff and stakeholders of the event.

Maps

Maps are a useful tool to present an event, particularly to contractors and equipment suppliers who may be required to setup at the site. The computer software programmes can be utilized to generate computer images to give a better understanding of the facility at the site to the different parties involved in the event. These parties might include the following:

- Designers
- Tally communications and electrical contractors
- Décor contractors
- Artists, entertainers, celebrities and exhibitors
- Event audience
- Access and exits for emergency response teams
- Access to emergency vehicles and fire tenders

Models

Models are also very useful, when most of client find it difficult to visualize three-dimensional presentation. A model can also assist in other aspects of event management such as crowd control and evacuation measures put in place. In such cases, some bottlenecks and some other problems may emerge from viewing a three-dimensional presentation. Most computer software can also present the information in a way that may allow the event manager and his team to anticipate all issues relating to design and implementation.

Gantt Charts

The Gantt Charts is an example of a fairly detailed level of planning. This chart is generally used in the early planning stage. In this type of planning, sheet and dates are listed across the top of the chart and rules (or blocks) illustrate how long each task listed in the char will take. This type of chart can clearly show the interdependence of different tasks of the event. Another aspect of this type of planning is to identify the critical path including those elements of the plan that are essential to the successful out come of the event. The general principle of identifying planning elements on which all else are dependent can be done with a Gantt chart.

In case of arrangements with sponsors, these need to be finalized before any work could be done on print or promotional materials to facilitate the sponsor to approve their logos. In case any sponsor pulls out of the arrangement, this change will have an impact on print production and promotional materials. Project planning software is available for specialized event. However, a spreadsheet may be sufficient for smaller events. The purpose is to identify the task, cluster them together and to choose the ideal level of details required in planning the event. The chart can also be expanded to the extent of showing even the smallest task of the event. The Gantt chart must be a user-friendly planning tool in order to prove effective.

At times a change in some part of event planning may be necessary and this significant change may make all available charts redundant. An experienced event manager can ascertain the level of planning required to ensure that every one is clear about his roles and responsibility, while remaining open to change.

A high level planning chart for an event provides a broad overview of the main event task with a general time line. Each of the major tasks in the high level planning chart could also be used as the basis for a more detailed plan. This may also show the planning process for recruiting and training staff for the preceding event, because the training aspects for the proposed event, is not covered fully in the Gantt chart. There would be many steps like writing training materials and seeking approval of the content from the different functional areas managers will be involved.

Run Sheets

The run sheet is also an essential tool for most event manager. It is the program or schedule of events. The run sheet is quite simple in the preliminary stages of planning with times allocation only for specific elements of the event. But as the planning progresses, the run sheet becomes more detailed with timings for staff, performers and technicians.

Finally a more detail run sheet can be developed, which is also called the script, to identify roles and cues of each person. Run sheets are one of the important tools for all stake holder and participants including the venue management team and subcontractors.

Organization Charts

An organization chart contains the staffing requirement for an event. It is another important tool used in planning an event. After all task have been identified and put in groups logically the staffing requirement for an event becomes clearer and can be put in an organization chart. This chart may help the people to understand their specific roles, avoiding any confusion.

The organization chart may be of three kinds; **Pre event charts, Charts during the Event and Post- event charts.** An organization chart can also include a brief list of task to be performed by each individual or the people performing each role. The chart clarifies roles and improves communication. It also contains a job description, outlining the tasks that need to be performed, is required for each role. This chart should also show the position title, the reporting relationship and the duties.

An event committee structure in an organizational chart:

Finance, Fundraising, Administration Committee

Publicity and Sponsorship Committees

Executive Committee

Facilities and Catering and Waste Committee

Operations Committee

Entertainment Committee

Courtesy: Event Management by Wagen and Carlos

Check Lists

A check list is a control tool that ensures that the individual staff performing the task has not forgotten a single detail. The check list is indispensable at the detailed level of planning. This is a part of the record-keeping process aim not only at preventive any potential problem, but also at reducing the risk of litigation if any thing goes wrong. Detailed and correctly implemented plans may reassure the client also, allow the event team to work effectively and build confidence in achieving the objectives of the event. It is also imperative that a specific checklist be followed and it be signed and dated on completion, especially in cases of checking emergency equipment like fire fighting equipment emergency exits.

It is necessary to spend sufficient time in planning and execution phase to make the event business more successful. In the event environment, things can turn bad in an instant and only a good planning can prevent this outcome from happening. If the plans have been thoughtfully developed, the role of the event manager remains simply to insure that the procedures are correctly implemented with minimal incidents and satisfied clients.

Safety Checklist

Name		Date and Time	
Task	Check	Comment	Follow up Required
First Aid kit fully equipped			
Flammable goods signage correct, Storage away from combustible materials			
Fire extinguisher visible, free of obstruction			
All electrical appliances tested			
Extension cords tested and tagged			
Extension cords not lying over walkways			
Boxes trash, etc not obstructing the excess or exit of emergency vehicles or fire fighting equipment			
Gas cut-off valve visible and obstruction free			

SUGGESTED QUESTIONS

1. How is an event conceptualized?
2. What are the elements of an event that impact an event conceptualization?
3. What is the role of an event expert in synchronizing different elements of an event?
4. How is a document designed?
5. What are the creative elements that are to be considered in designing an event?
6. How is the concept of an event analyzed and evaluated?
7. What do you mean by planning an event?
8. What are needs and advantages of event planning?
9. What are the different stages of planning process?
10. What are different tools of event planning?

8

SAFETY AND SECURITY OF EVENTS

Safety of Events

Safety of the event audience, staff and subcontractors should be of paramount concern for every event manager, since all events carry safety risks that may result in anything from accidents to the evacuation of venue. We will look at the potential for injury being caused by fixed or temporary structures, which may in turn be subjected to damage.

Another issue for consideration for most events is that of line management. Lines can be managed very well or very badly. The delays getting into events, such as many sporting events or concerts, are sometimes so bad that the event manager has to direct its staff to stop collecting ticket and simply and open gates for every one. Clearly, any such situation can lead to problems inside the venue if the people without ticket to manage to enter inside the venue. On the other hand if the sporting event has commenced, and perhaps points have been scored, while the spectators remain outside there would be little left that could be done. However, if there were a number of people without tickets outside the venue, this may not be a viable option.

Then the orderly management of spectators leaving the venue is also equally important. Clear directions and signage are necessary to guide the spectator to public transportation and parking. Sometimes, spectators enjoy themselves so much at the event venue that they have to be taken out by security staff.

Security of Events

Security is generally required for premises, equipment, cash, and other valuable materials. But the predominant role of most event security staff is to ensure that the genuine People have the excess to specific areas and to act responsibly in case of any accident or emergency. Identification badges, like a tag hanging around the neck showing the areas to which they (staff, media or spectator area) have access, and allow security staff to monitor access. Ejection of people who are behaving unruly- sometimes with the cooperation of police personnel, as and when necessary.

There are several considerations in the organization of security for an event. First, it is necessary to calculate the number of trained staff required for security job. If the venue covers a large area, vehicles and equipment may also be required for security staff. And finally the level of threat will determine whether fire arms are also required. In all cases, security staff should be appropriately licensed and the security company should carry the required insurance.

Police Service

Local police departments often provide some of the required services at a limited or no cost for community events. However, with the growth of event industry and the increased demands on police for spectator control, some charges are being levied by police departments for the forces deployed for an event. The number of police personnel required is negotiated by the event manager and the police department and the number is decided by the history of incidents associated with similar events and nature of the event.

Security Services

With the growth of security service agency and availability of trained security personnel, the services of security service can also be utilized. The event industry is regulated under certain rule and the event organizer must ensure that the required licenses are obtained. There are various classes of licensing requirements for individual security officers specially deputed with arms. All security officer related to the event management industry are required to undergo a criminal record check through police verification.

The roles of security officer related to the event management industry include the following:

- Acting as bodyguard, bouncer, or crowd controller
- Patrolling or protecting premises
- Installing and maintaining security equipment
- Providing advice on security equipment and procedures
- Training staff on security procedure

Security service agency must posses appropriate general liability insurance coverage. General liability insurance coverage is, in fact, a requirement of almost all contracts between the event organizer and subcontractors. Subcontractors including security service agency are also required to cover their staff for work related to health and safety incident.

Other Security Related Considerations

- Verification of location of all underground or embedded electrical circuits before digging or cutting
- To find out the reason of any operated fuse or tripping of circuit breaker before replacing or resetting them
- To find out where the over current devises such as circuit breaker and fuses are located so that they can be easily and quickly reached in case of any emergency
- Before replacing lamps and bulbs, verify that the replacement matches fixture requirements

Safe Use of Machinery

There are a number of machinery hazards. The use of machinery may result in serious injuries and fatalities. Many factors can cause or increase the risk, such as using the wrong machinery poor maintenance of machinery and inadequate training in the use of machinery there are several control measures to ensure the safe use of machinery. These include using the right equipment, providing machinery guards, providing maintenance and cleaning staff and training and supervision of machine operator.

Handling of Hazardous Materials

Because different chemicals have different safe use requirement, it is necessary for staff deployed to know fully about hazarders material used at the work place. Material safety data sheets should be used to provide to staff members with the following advices on these materials:

- Ingredients of a product
- Health hazard and first/aid instruction
- Precautions for use
- Safe handling and storage information
- Emergency procedure

Fire-fighting Precautions

Sufficient numbers of fire control devices should be installed at vital places with the aid and advice of Fire-fighting department officers. The nearest Fire Service Station should also be kept informed by the event organizers, specially having in mind the presence of any inflammable materials, if any, present at the event site.

Safety Signs

Safety signs guide the staff to move towards the desire direction at the event work place. Safety signs are especially important, since staffs are generally for a short period at the event work place. This does not allow much time for the training of staff about safety issues however safety issue and safety precautions may be stressed during the brief sessions of the staff. Safety poster and safety signs can be used to reinforce key messages regarding safety, which can help to prevent accidents. Signs should be also put directing the visitors towards public transport and parking spots.

First Aid

Event managers need to alert local authorities; police, fire services departments, ambulance services, about the planned event. At the same time venue and event staff should also be trained in first-aid procedures and the use of fire fighting equipment put in place at the event venue. Some of these procedure will be specific to an event. For example at a marathon race, common emergencies that may occur and require first-aid, may include exhaustion, collapse dehydration, bone and muscle injury etc. Procedures and necessary first-aid should be put in place to deal with these emergency and other anticipated ones. Sometimes, participants in such races do not want to accept help and event staffs are required to be trained in the correct procedure to deal with any such occurrence.

Incident Communication

For any event, there are certain standard and well-structured reporting system on all operational issues. These reporting systems should be a part of the organization chart. However many instances have happened when communication system was found less formal and less structured. It has often happened in the case of "mayhem" or "controlled chaos." Communication system relating to an incident or emergency, in one and all cases, needs to be very clear and well devised, tried and tested. It must also follow a short and specific chain of command. The chain of command and the organization chart for an emergency is seldom the same, for the event as a whole. Emergency reporting tends to go through very few levels, but all staff must be trained in emergency reporting. The staff involved in this task are general staff, security staff first-aid staff, police and emergency services including fire-fighting staff. Absolute clarity is needed as to who takes key decision and how they are to be contacted.

Implementation of Emergency Procedures

In order to implement emergency procedures effectively, the following action should be taken:

- Review Implementation procedure and integrate with overall event operational plans.
- Ensure complete awareness of the procedure among all concerned, by disseminating information and wide consultations.
- Provide required information through the use of signage and designed communication materials.
- Trained all staff about their role in emergency.
- Rehearsals of conducting evacuation exercises.
- Review and make necessary changes in the procedures to ensure its effectiveness.
- Study the Action Taken Report of previous events under different crises.

Fire Procedures

Normally the following steps should be taken in case of any fire at the event venue:

- Ensure the safety of every one within the vicinity of the fire.
- Call the Fire Services department in case of any expansion of fire.
- Start immediately, the evacuation in accordance with evacuation procedures.
- Fight the fire with the available fire extinguisher cylinders and other available equipment or retreat and close all doors

Evacuation Procedures

A crisis management plan relies on the chain of command and an early warning system for a fast intervention. During the evacuation certain personal traits and characters are required to be shown by all staff:

- Remain calm.
- Be observant.
- Listen to and follow all instructions strictly and diligently.
- Provide all information and instruction to all staff and spectators.
- Follow all safety precautions laid down for such situations.

Communication Method

There should be a well laid out information system for every event. Most events teams use radios, since they are the most effective and dependable tool for communication. For this, it is essential that the correct radio procedure be followed. Event operations center is with control serving as the link to the decision maker.

But now- a- days cell phones are more in use. The draw back of this system of communication is that the information can be overheard. Networks can also become overloaded if spectators are also using their cell phone, especially during intermission and at the end of the concert.

Event Risks Management

Event organizers often think risk in terms of safety and security, but risk is much broader than the concept of safety and security. Risk is the chance that something will-may go wrong at the time of staging the event. It may include a cash-flow crises, a staff strike, a fire and of course, weather. Even if it does not have a direct impact on the event, bad weather will reduce the number of spectators at an event unless adequate protection from bad weather is provided. Rainy or stormy weather also casts its impact on the mood of the people and can play a spoil spot in motivating the spectators. Event managers require a careful planning to save off any such situation. Risk management is the process of identifying, assessing and managing these risks.

Process of Risk Management

The process of event management involves three steps:

(I) Identifying risks and hazards

(II) Assessing the risks and hazards
(III) Managing the risks and hazards

This process enables the event organizer to establish and prioritize the risks, to take steps to prevent any such problems from occurring and to make contingency plans to tide over the problems, if they occur.

Identifying the Risks and Hazards of the Event

The first step is to identify the risks or hazard and ascertaining when and how any such problem can occur. The next step is to analyze the likelihood of the problem to arise and its probable consequences. For example, a mismanagement by any poor performance by junior staff of the event management team could probably be managed and resolved without consequences. But any mismanagement by a senior staff, for instance, responsible for sponsorship could have dire consequences.

Some of the hazards that may prove as potential risks include the following:

- Fire
- Equipment
- Electrical equipment
- Storing of hazardous substances
- Spills
- Stacking of unbalanced heavy equipment and items
- Temporary fencing, temporary stages and other venue furniture
- Accidents of vehicles

A detailed discussion among the members of the event management team may help to identify potential risks. A detailed lists of possible problems and a research in the material and information, including all legislative requirements and conversations with organizers and experienced manager of similar event are required to identify the possible risks.

Assessing the Risks and Hazards of the Event

After identifying the potential risks and hazards, the likelihood of occurring needs to be assessed. In this process the team will prioritize the issues for attention. A committee should be setup to manage risks safety and security issues and operational guide lines for equipment, their testing schedules and the like needs to be formulated. The following factor should be considered, for example in case of heavy rain:

- What is the likelihood of the risks apprehended?
- Who will be exposed to the risk?
- What impact had this risk in similar circumstances in any earlier event?
- How the spectators and staff of the event management team will react to the risk- hazard?

The hazards related to health and safety may be different types of injuries. It is also to be assessed whether the nature of injuries is fatal/ grievous injury, serious injury/ illness or moderate injury or illness. The potential consequences of fire, flood, bones and computer failure can also be evaluated in the same manner.

Managing the Risks and Hazards of the Event

After prioritizing the risks and hazards, the final step will be to find out the most effective and possible ways of managing the risks. The measures to be taken may include the following:

- Elimination plans to eliminate the risk altogether.
- Constitute plans.
- Isolation plan for isolating dangerous equipment
- Engineering controls for using safety barriers and to control crowds
- Administrative controls like erecting warning signage and putting the trained staff well in procedures
- Contingency plans like evacuation plans etc.

However the following risks need to be considered seriously by any event planner:

Natural Disasters

Heavy rain is a disaster for an outdoor event, as too are hail, snow, and extreme heat. Freak acts of nature such as hurricanes and tornadoes can land amuck in the middle of an event. According to a report in USA Today, "A rare tornado touched down without warning Wednesday in down-town Salt Lake City, killing one person and injuring more than 100. The black, swirling cloud struck about 1p.m., uprooting trees and temporary buildings set up for a retailer's convention." Flooding can affect event venues, particularly temporary ones, and it can also cause damage to electrical wiring-potentially a very serious risk. Of course, fire is one of the risks that most venue managers fear and must plan for, since evacuation of large crowd is extremely difficult.

Financial Risk

Financial risk may involve unforeseen costs, lower than expected revenue, high exchange rates, general decline in economic circumstances and disposable income, fraud committed by any stakeholder fines imposed by any legal authority or cash-flow problems.

Technology- Related Risks

Technological failure is an increasing risk for high profile events. This happens more in such event which are relatively more reliant on computer programming and computer networks operating successfully. For example, this problem may happen with guest registration at a trade exhibition and would prevent the records of attendee data, which are essential information for any exhibitor. For an exhibition organizer, the attendance list generated during registration, is his most valuable assets. It would be met available to participating exhibiters, who want to follow up the contacts with the attendee who are generally potential buyers of the items put in the exhibition. The event organizer may also use it in the advertising drive for the next event of similar nature.

Mismanagement

A good management is an essential requirement of a successful event. A good management requires detailed planning and sound interpersonal relationship at all levels. Mismanagement can hinder an event organizer from achieving their objectives. The people related problems, such as disputes at the top management levels, can lead to the dismissal of key staff. Both of these are potential risks in managing an event successfully.

Safety and Security Risk

Accidents riots, terrorism and sabotage are all safety and security risks. Safety and security measure have been described in detail in this chapter earlier.

Risk at Sports Events

The risks associated with most community, commercial and entertainment events are normally financial. However, with sporting events, there is the additional risk of danger to the participants and in some cases to the audience. There are numerous examples of audience frenzy during the football matches between different European football clubs, when there was a scene of riots between the supporter of wining and losing teams and it resulted into casualties in many cases. The challenges for the organizer of such events are to reduce the risk to an acceptable levels by careful planning and by introducing new procedures and technology, where and when available. Safety standards changed over. Working out the safety standards for a particular sporting event at a particular time involves looking at a particular factor. One of these may be out of the following:

- Perceived level of acceptable risks of participants and audience.
- Current legislation and legal precedents.
- Availability of risk management solutions.
- Development and implementation of plans, procedures and control mechanisms

The last of the above mention factors is extremely important for event organizers. If the organizer can show their procedures for managing risk were well considered and well implemented, such a planning would stand them in good stead in case of any charge of negligence is leveled against them.

Another important risk issue for event organizers is concerned with temporary fencing, temporary stage or seating. There have been the cases of a number of accidents where temporary seating stands collapsed at a special event, resulting in injury to participants and audience. The services of a structural engineer should be taken when temporary fencing, stage or seating is used. It is also necessary to take steps to ensure that proper and correct safety standards are being met.

Incident Reporting

Incident reporting is an important risk control process, and it is essential that every member of the event team is familiar with this process. An incident report card should be completed for every problem that occurs, from customer complaints to slips and falls. On receipt of the incident report cards, management staff can look for patterns in the incidents and for ways in which these risks can be better managed.

There are several reasons for maintaining all documentation relating to risk

- To demonstrate that an appropriate process was in place
- To provide a record of incidents and responses
- To allow monitoring, review and improvement

The result of such an approach may result in the following:

- Reduction in problems, incidents and accidents
- Improvement in legislative/legal compliance
- Decrease in liability
- Improvement in work place performance
- Customers' satisfaction

- Avoidance of negative media exposures and other controversial issues

Emergency Response Plans

Every event or venue should have an emergency response plan (ERP). ERP is usually developed in collaboration with professional consultant who also train staff on procedures and involvement of every one engaged in the event, including in evacuation plans and procedures. A simple risk management plan shows the anticipated risks, the potential impact of such risks and management strategy including contingency plans put in place to control them.

Risk Management Apparatus

Risk management is an integral part of good management practices. It is an iterative process consisting of steps to be taken in sequence, in order to enable continual improvement in the decision making.

An Accident Report Card

Date	Name of the person reporting	Time Position held	Functional area/ Department

Names of persons involved in the incident

Names and contact details of witnesses, if any

Incident details

Name of the Incident
Location of the Incident
Cause of the incident
Consequences of the Incident
Can any action be taken to prevent recurrence?
Date and time received and logged
Outstanding actions

SUGGESTED QUESTIONS

1. What is the importance of safety for an event manager?
2. What are the main considerations in organizing of security for an event?
3. Draw a chart for implementation of emergency procedure for staging an event.
4. What is the event risk management?
5. What are main steps to be taken in the process of risk management in an event?
6. What are the measures to be taken in managing the risk and hazards of the event?
7. How is an emergency risk plan developed?
8. Prepare an accident report card.

9

STAGGING AND EXECUTION OF EVENT

Event management is actually the backbone of any enterprise. It is the flow of events that describes and defines various activities in an enterprise for the present and the future. Corporate events, conferences, seminars, live concerts etc are an integral part of the communication strategy of an enterprise. Events are now specialized in nature, organized and planned in a manner which could turn the event into a successful exercise.

During the incident response phase, the real time-tracking of incident and response resources are critical. Events planners welcome guest, answer doors, provide food and beverage service, clean up and do a number of other chores. Producing a successful event requires savvy production skill highly detailed planning and complete integration.

The staging of an event comprises all aspects of the event that enable the performance to go ahead smoothly and successfully. Broadly speaking, the performance means entertainment, the sport, the parade and the ceremony. Theme, venue, sound, light and all other essential services are necessary for events and festival. Capacity, seating arrangement, emergency access, and emergency exists, stage requirement and staffing are all to be looked into diligently and carefully.

Selection of Event Site

Selection of event site must take into account of all stakeholders. These stakeholders may include emergency service, catering staff, entertainers, participants, audience and clients. The selection of the site must be based on a rational decision making and not on any imaginative idea. An existing event venue such as conference center, exhibition place could more easily be transformed using decoration and crops, than an open space such as a parking lot or a playground. Selection venue must be consistent with the event purpose and theme. It may prove cost saving, since it requires far less expenses in transforming it into, a suitable one to the needs and wants of the client.

The major considerations for the selection of an event venue may include the following:

- Layout of the site and its suitability to the size of the event.
- Stage and performance area
- Transport and parking
- Proximity to accommodation
- Space for service providers, such as caterers
- Technical support
- Compatibility with event theme
- Audience comfort, specially for seating, entrances and exits
- Visibility for the audience
- Safety and security
- Access of emergency vehicles/services
- Evacuations routes

Stakeholders of Event

There are three major stakeholders in viewing a suitable event site; **the performers, audience and the organizers.** Performers have specific requirements that are fundamental to their success, such as the level of intimacy. The audience's primary requirements are to see and hear what is going on. The level of light and sound and comforts in seating, also contribute to the satisfaction of the audience. From the organizer's perspective the venue must minimize the risk, such as adverse weather, accidents and emergencies.

Support for the Theme

The theme of an event must be supported in every aspect, including special effect. A theme can be developed and reinforced through some creative elements. Some of them are the following:

Color, landscape and/or location, humor, entertainment and fantasy. The event organizer must carefully consider some aspects of the theme like décor, entertainment, layout, lighting, sound, vision, stage, set, performance area and other special effects.

Entertainment companies can look at the event theme and come up with a range of concepts to suit the theme after familiarizing themselves with the event purpose and event audience. Décor encompasses many things from the color scheme to the drapes, props and floral arrangements. Staging rental companies can be helpful with the tasks and challenges to bring them all together into a cohesive theme. The layout of the event venue is integral to the success of the event. Layout is required to be negotiated with the client well in advance. While planning an event in which guests are seated around a table, it is essential to plan the lay out accordingly.

Lighting can be used both to create a general ambiance and highlight a particular feature. Light is often synchronized with sound for special effects at dances and firework displays. Light with sound, is used to create a particular mood, of course in consistent with the event theme. Music volume needs to be pitched at just the right level and all members of the audience need to hear clearly, both sitting near and far from the stage, particularly when the event is being organized in a stadium.

Vision incorporates all projected images such as relays of sporting highlights on large screens or score boards. Video projectors, slide projectors can project images onto screens for dramatic effect and to be extended to live telecasts with satellite links.

Stage is used for performances, prize giving and presentations. But the needs of the audience is the most important considerations, particularly the line of sight. The set includes all objects on the stage;

props flats, lecterns, stairs, curtains and so on. The cyclorama is the drape at the back of the stage used to create a sense of distance, special lighting of the cyclorama providing different colored backgrounds. Legs (vertical) and teasers (horizontal) are used to mask part of the rigging system and to trim the sightlines so that only the set may be seen by the audience. A traveler is a type of curtain that moves along a track. It is often used as the main stage curtain.

Each sporting event has specific requirements. Line of sight is more important for sporting enthusiasts and visibility from every seat for which ticket has been sold, is a must. The placement of media equipment should be predetermined, especially the position of cameras and sound equipment before tickets are sold. The elevated position of camera crews is preferred to cover processions and parades. Finally giant screens with rear screen projector are considered for the use for venues, specially where it is doubted that members of the audience may not be able to see comfortably the stage or the field of the play.

Conducting Rehearsals

The importance of rehearsals can hardly be overemphasized. This is the opportunity for all involved to integrate the efforts; every one from the stage manager to the technical support staff. A technical run-through allows the staff involved to test the setup and to make sure that all elements work satisfactorily. Technical glitches at an event are unprofessional, to say the least, so a backup plan for all aspects of the presentation is absolutely is essential. This includes copies of each video or sound clip, slide presentation in more than one format and multiple microphones. Every potential and expected problem should have a ready solution. The final aspect is the quality of the presentation given by the speaker particularly at business and academic conferences.

Provision of Services

The supply of water, power and gas; a communication network and efficient transport and traffic management is essential for the staging of successful events.

Essential Services

Essential services include power, water and gas. The choice of a complex site can add to the difficulties of providing these essential services to the event venue.

Communication Network

Many events have special requirements for communication which may even include the installation of a complete telephone and communication network. A stadium often requires its own mobile phone base station on account of the number of people using mobile telephone particularly at end of the event.

Transportation and Traffic Management

Transportation to the event, including air, rail, bus and taxi, all need to be considered. In addition the issue of the parking and its impact on local traffic are also to be considered. Thoughts must also be given to access for people with disabilities, marshaling of crowds, especially after the event is over, and notifying of business affected by any disruption.

Catering Services

A catering contractor usually does the catering for an event, taking care of food orders, food production and service staff. These contractors should provide menus and costs relevant to the style of service required. Photographs of previous catering and food presentations styles can be helpful in making a decision. Food that is prepared off-site and heated or deep-fried on site can be very cost effective as long as safe food handling practices are followed. While discussing catering contracts, the event organizer needs to be very explicit about food qualities, speed of service, and food requirement. A food safety plan is another essential item when planning an event. Food safety involves protecting the customer from food poisoning by implementing a plan to prevent cross-contamination and other factors that cause bacterial growth. For example food needs to be kept at the correct temperature all the way from the factory or the market to the store, into the kitchen and to the buffet. Food safety plans look at every aspect of food handling and, if implemented properly, may ensure the measurement of temperatures at key points in the process in accordance with the guidelines of the plan. The best kitchens have refrigerated delivery areas and separate storage for vegetables, meat, seafood and other products at the correct temperatures. Planned food production processes, including plating food in a refrigerated area, can further reduce the risk of bacterial growth.

Catering for an event is extremely demanding for those in the kitchen. Producing several hundred hot meals is not for the weak-hearted persons. The Chef should be aware of the planned time service of all courses and this should be conferred at an early stage of the planning. Most floor managers will ask the Chief, how much notice is needed for service of the main course and they will monitor proceedings and advise the Chief accordingly.

Organizing Accommodations

For many conferences, exhibitions, shows and sporting event organizations, accommodations are an integral part of the package. The packaging of air travel and accommodations demand that planning for such events occur well in advance in orderly room rates. If such rate reductions are essential to favorable pricing of the event, it is preferable to hold the event in an off-peak season.

Managing the Environment

Waste management is an important consideration for all event organizers. Method for reducing the environmental impact of noise, air and water pollution should be part of the planning process and necessary advice on these matters can be obtained from the Environment Protection Agency which has offices in each state.

Professional contractors can advise you on the correct disposal of cooking oils and others toxic waste that could affect our water supply. Clearly marked bins should be provided to facilitate recycling of waste products. With regard to air pollution, releasing helium balloons into the atmosphere has been shown to be environmentally unfriendly and therefore, this practice is slowly dieing out around the world.

Restroom Facilities

Restroom facilities include those facilities at the venue and any other temporary facilities required. The number and type of toilets to be provided at the event venue including the number allocated to men, women and people with disabilities, is another part of the decision making process. It is essential to discuss requirements for any event that the organizer is planning with a rest room facilities rental company, since they are the experts.

Cleaning Arrangement

There are a number of such cleaning contractors who specialize in cleaning during events. In most cases cleaning is done before and after the event. Maintaining cleanliness during peak times is a challenging job, particularly if there is only a short changeover time between events sessions. In that case the organizer has to get one audience out, cleaning and replenishment of stocks done and the next audience in no time. Cleaning staff should be treated as part of the event staff and given appropriate training, so that they can answer the questions from the people attending the event.

So the staging of an event involves a myriad of tasks for the event organizer. With some events, staging process may even include managing the fans that wait in line for days before the event to meet the artiste at the event places. For example, at the Academy Awards the area designated for fans, is occupied for weeks together before the big night, since one of the fans receives a free grand stand seat overlooking the red carpet. According to London Daily Telegraph (April 20, 2001), "The commitment of Oscar followers makes Wimbledon campers look like amateurs. A thriving industry has developed around their needs, from food stands to camping equipment."

Staging an event is probably the most creative aspect of event management, and there is enormous scope for making an event memorable by using the best combination of staging elements. The selection of the right site for an event is necessary, since this can have an enormous impact on the staging of the event and the level of creativity that can be employed in developing the theme.

SUGGESTED QUESTION

1. What are the factors to be taken into consideration while selecting an event sight?
2. Who are the major stakeholders of an event?
3. How do other factors veer round the theme of the event?
4. What is the importance of rehearsals before staging an event?
5. What are the essential services required for staging an event?
6. Staging an event is probably the most creative aspect of an event management. Explain.

10

Staff Pattern, Recruitment and Training

Staff Pattern and Organization Chart

Organization planning for events generally requires several organization charts, one each for different stage and different task. For this it is necessary to develop the organization chart and specification and descriptions of jobs are required to be clearly delineated. This will help to recruit and select proper type of staff and train them according to their job specification. It is also necessary to devise staffing policy and manage industrial relations. It is also necessary to draw a communication system and policy and understand the needs of spectators. The organization chart should be developed in such way that people should understand their specific roles and their reporting relationships in order to avoid any confusion in this regard.

Pre-event Charts

Prier to the event, the focus is on planning and drawing the chart. The pre-event charts required during the period of show should include the following

- All those responsible for the primary functions during the planning stage, such as finance, marketing, entertainment, catering security, liaising with statutory authorities etc. The core event management team for a local festival may include Festival Director, Marketing Manager, Executive and Coordinator, Ticketing Manager, Artist Coordinator and Producer.

- Small cross-functional teams to manage specific issues such as security and safety and customer service.
- Stakeholder committee, including of contractors, suppliers and public bodies.

Charts during the Event

The size of the organization generally increases by the time the event is organized and the requirements of a full scale operation should be taken into account while finalizing the staffing levels. Charts for the event should draw the following:

- Full staff chart along with reporting relationships for the over all event operations, both during normal functioning and in cases of emergency as well.
- Emergency reporting relationship should be more simplified for a quick response.

Post Event Charts

Normally after the event the team disperses and is left with only a few staff. An organization chart can also include a short list of task to be performed by individual and the people performing each role. Such a list mentions clearly the roles of different staff and improves the communication system and its efficient functioning, especially during emergency.

Outlining Job Descriptions

A job description outlines the task that need to be performed and required for each role. The document should show the position title, the reporting system and the duties. A position summery may also be put in the chart. In addition to the sections mentioned in the job description, there should be a paragraph showing the terms and condition of employment, salary applicable, where as those for some other position would show the award and the pay rate under the award. Since this position is likely to be a temporary one, the job description should also show the period of engagement. The experience of the managing subcontractors will be the guiding factors in selecting organization for the catering contracts and other contracts. Managing the supply of products promised in the contracts would be an essential consideration.

Once the job description is complete it is necessary to develop a specification for each person. This will identify the skills, knowledge and experience required for the role to be entrusted. The experience in a similar role would be required along with the experience of contract management. In addition, knowledge of menu planning and costing would be essential as would be the knowledge of food hygiene planning. For the requirements for a position, experience in an event management is desirable. However the experience in managing multiple contracts, such as in a resort, hotel or catering organization may be relevant in the absence of formal event management experience.

A Sample of Job Description could be like this

Job Description

Position title: Catering Services Manager
Reports to: Venue Services Manager
Responsible for: Sub- contracts with caterers/concessionaires

Position summary: To meet the food and beverage needs of all customer groups through the selection and management of appropriate subcontractors and concessionaires. To ensure compliance with the negotiated agreements regarding menus, pricing, quality and service.

Duties:

- Develop contracts for provision of food and beverage, including bars, fast food, coffee kiosks, snack bars, VIP and staff catering.
- Select subcontractors and confirm agreements regarding menus, pricing, staffing and service levels.
- Develop operational procedures with special attention to integration of services, food hygiene plans, supply and storage of food and beverage, staffing and waste management.
- Work with venue operations on the installation of the required facilities and essential services (power, water and gas) for food and beverages outlets.
- Monitor performance of contractors.
- Deal with daily operational and customer issues.

Source: Event Management by Wagon and Carlos

Recruitment

The common approach to recruitment is to advertise the position in local or national newspapers, on the Internet home page for the event or the event related sites. Employment agency can also provide event staff for a placement fee. The employment agency can cut down your work by providing a short list of suitable applicants and manage the administrative work of employment.

Engagement of Volunteers

The best places to look for volunteers are volunteer organization, schools, colleges and universities. While selecting paid or honorary volunteer staff, their suitability for the job should be checked and ensured. In case of any position the recruitment officer could focus on for example, food safety procedures and licensing, since both are relevant to the position of a catering services manager.

A Sample of Job description and specification of a catering services manager

Job description

Title of the post: Catering Services manager
Reporting to: Venue Services manager
Responsibility: Sub-contractors with caterers

Position Summary: To meet the food and beverage needs of all customer groups through the selection and management of suitable subcontractors. To ensure compliance with the negotiated agreement regarding menus, pricing quality and service.

Rosters for Staff

Staff planning includes the drawing of work rosters, especially if multiple sessions and multiple days are involved and interrelated tasks have to be considered, as sufficient time needs to be factored in for each task. In the event management there is often limited time from transition from one session to the next, and there are many interrelated jobs to be done requiring detailed planning and scheduling. A staffing problem in the hours preceding an event can also contribute to the risk of accidents and poor service.

Training of Event Staff

Training of event staff is a necessity in view of sensitiveness of the event management. It is also required to fine-tune the staff to the specific job especially in human relation. The training of event staff is essential in three basic areas: (i) **the objective of event (ii) the venue of event and (iii) their specific duties.**

General Outline of the Objectives

Staff members are required to be presented with a general outline of the objectives of event and organizational structure they need to be motivated to provide satisfactory service and reliable services to every member of the event audience.

Venue Information

The staff should be taken a round of the event venue to enable them to familiarize them selves with the location of all facilities, functional areas and services provided for the spectators. This also includes the time to cover all emergency procedures.

Specific Duty Information

Event staff members need to know what their duties are and how they will perform them. Maps and check lists can be very useful for these purposes. Rehearsals and information about role-playing help the staff to familiarize with their roles before the event audience.

The training has to focus on the more general aspects, and move from the general to specific, which is personally more relevant. This is all the more necessary in cases where access to the venue is permitted only at the last minute. Team building activities such as games and competition should be included in all training which may help develop relationships. Event leaders need to accelerate all processes in order to hold the attention of the trainees and develop team sprit.

On the conclusion of the training, the event manager should be confident that all staff members have achieved training objectives. Training materials need to be prepared in a user-friendly, simple language and jargon-free format for participants. The following check list covers the information to be included in training manuals and training sessions:

- Location of check in area and check in procedure
- Reporting for shift and briefing
- Uniform and equipment
- Supervision
- Specific roles

- Breaks and meals
- Debriefing and check-out
- Venue organization and support operations
- Staffing roles
- Emergency procedures
- Other relevant procedures
- Event objective
- Event audience expectation
- Transportation
- Local service information
- Contingency planning

As a general principle customer service training is essential for quality service. For this the focus should be on specific information required by staff in order to assists properly to customer. Most event staff rate specific event information for the event audience as the most relevant to their training needs.

Staff Briefing

Briefing of staff is an extension of the training period and allows the venue or event manager to impart relevant information to staff before they commence work in every shift. Some information may be new whereas other elements may be reinforcements of key information such as incident reporting or emergency procedure.

Developing Recognition Strategies

Recognition of the work of both paid and volunteer staff can have a huge impact on motivation. One of the most effective strategies is the development of realistic goals for staff because this allows individuals to see that their work has contributed to the success of event.

Intangible reward includes the following:

- goal achieved through individual and team targets and competitions

- job rotation
- job enrichments
- meeting athletes, stars, musicians and artists
- working with people from overseas
- providing service and information and performing other meaningful tasks
- praise and verbal recognition
- training and skill development
- opportunities for building relationship and friendship
- media recognition

Tangible rewards include:

- merchandise
- tickets
- post event parties
- recognition certificates
- statement of duties performed
- meals and uniforms of a high standard
- badges, memorabilia

Linking performance to individual or team goals should be considered carefully for motivating staff. When recognition is given to individuals, it may cause accusations of inequity. Team motivations are more likely to improve team performance and also develop camaraderie.

Managing Volunteers

Volunteer management is particularly relevant to the event business, since many events are staffed by volunteers. The following list offers suggestions for training and treating volunteers:

- Volunteers have the rights to be treated as co-workers.
- They should be allocated a suitable assignments, task or job.
- They should know the purpose and rules of the organization.

- In addition to guidance and direction they should receive continuing education.
- They should be provided a working place, proper tools and required materials.
- Volunteers should also be allowed to offer suggestions and be heard.
- At the end of event they should be issued a reference letter.

The following are expected from volunteers:

- They should also put in same effort and service, as a paid worker does.
- They should give proper work performance and maintain equal punctuality and reliability enthusiasm and work culture.
- Loyalty to the organization is also expected from them.
- They should communicate clearly.

The works performed by volunteers generally include as the following:

- Customer relations officer.
- Protocol/public relations officer.
- First aid officer.
- Medical assistant.
- Security officer.
- Safety officer.
- Information officer.
- Time keeper.
- Shift coordinator, and others

In return volunteers get a number of personal benefits. Some of them may be the following:

- Social contact.
- Personal satisfaction of doing some thing worthwhile.
- Learning new skills.
- Using skills and experience.
- Helping others in the community.

Volunteers offer their services mainly for social contact and being active. They also receive reward in the form of merchandise. They also get opportunities to meet renowned musicians, sport personality and celebrities associated with the event. Some volunteers offer their services for a cause in being part of the event. The achievement of specific service targets given to them give them a short of self satisfaction and a motivation for both paid and volunteer staff.

During Winter Olympic Games, 8,000 volunteers for programme activities, 18,000 core volunteers for the Games and 6,000 volunteers for the Paralympics. Winter Games were engaged by Salt Lack Olympic Committee. These volunteers were engaged to assist in running the mega event.

Staffing is a very important part of event management and is crucial to the smooth and successful running of an event. Recruitment and selection of staff help to bring them for the job and induction and training prepared them for their specified jobs in the event. Most importantly, the event manager is required to be able to manage the event as also to mange industrial relations and to look into occupational health and safety issue.

SUGGESTED QUESTIONS

1. What is the importance of staff chart in an organization planning?
2. How should an organization chart be drawn for the successful staging of an event?
3. What are the requirements of a pre-event chart?
4. How does the chart during the event differ from pre-event charts?
5. Who should be included in post event chart?
6. Draw an outline of job description of an event manager.
7. What is the relevance of volunteer's management in the event business?
8. Write short notes on
   (a) Pre-event chart
   (b) During the event chart, and
   (c) Post event chart

11

Crowd Management and Evacuation Strategy

For any event management, contingency plans need to be in place in case of emergencies at an event venue and an easy access for emergency services needs to be considered. The evacuation in case of emergency like fire, etc and crowd management, specially after the event is over, are required to be put in place essentially.

The initial task of the event manager is to develop a crowd management plan.

The Crowd Management Plan

The following are the key things to consider when developing this type of plan:

- The number of people at the venue (the event audience, staff and contractors).
- The likely behavior of the spectator, with the experience of crowd behavior problems arisen in past.
- The timing of the event.
- The lay out of the venue.
- The security arrangements provided.
- Other general guideline, including about occupational health, safety rules and exit rules etc.

The crowd management plan covers available information such as the dimensions of the event venue or the site. It also covers the probable number of spectators at particular times of the event and their flow through the site. The peak periods are the most problematic from a crowd management perspective. A suitable plans needs to be put in place to address the challenges arising out of the following:

- Estimate the number of attendance for specific day and time.
- Estimate the number of people using public corridors, specific entrances and seating at a particular time.
- Estimate the number of ushers and service and security personnel required for crowd management.
- Requirements for crowd control measure such as barriers and rallying in front of the gate to regulate the entrance and exit of the crowd in queue.
- Identify the areas to be restricted.
- Develop a system for restricted access by specific staff.
- Identify particular hazards.
- Identify the access routes for emergency service personnel.
- Develop a foolproof system of communication and information for all staff working on the site.
- Establish a chain of command for incident reporting.
- Check safety equipment, such as number of fire extinguishers etc.
- Identify the safety requirements of different groups of people such as children, disables, players and performers.
- Make provision for first-aid requirements.
- Develop an Emergency Response Plan.
- Develop an evacuation plan and training programme for staff concerned.

There are many types of event venue, each having specific features and different safety requirements. However a crowd management and evacuation plan would be required to be developed for each event held at the venue, depending on factors such as crowd number and movement.

Major Risks

The major risks that are required to be considered in relation to the crowd management and evacuation during any event may include the following:

- Fire, smoke or gas leakages.
- Bomb threat, terrorism or specific threat to any VIP.
- Flood, earthquake or any other natural calamities.
- Crowd crush, overcrowding, congestion.
- Riots, protests.
- Haste ness on the part of the spectators to exit specially after the event is over.
- Collapse of structures or the fences of the event venue.
- Vehicle accidents.

The procedures should be in place for the emergency team to prevent panic among the public. Reassuring messages should be given on prearranged public address system to reduce panic and ensure orderly evacuation of all spectators.

Crowd Management

After identifying the range of risks, the circumstance that may lead to bad or destructive behavior in these contacts need to be analyzed. Depending on the nature of different risks, they need to be prioritized and necessary plan to put in place to avoid them as preventive measures or to deal with them should they occur, under contingency measures. Damage to property by spectators also needs to be covered and required procedure put in place for ejecting the offending spectators. The more serious risk lies from non-ticked spectators who get illegal entry.

The following strategies may help to prevent damages to fans during large events:

- Review the behavior of crowds attending similar past events.
- Review crowd responses to specific bands and performers at past rock concerts.

- Obtain engineering and specialist advice.
- Station special first-aid assistance.
- Provide specially trained private security and "peer security."
- Pad the floor and all hard surfaces, including barriers and railings.

Emergency Planning

Every business needs to have guidelines for emergencies that impact normal workplaces operations. The guidelines should include communication protocols and evacuation procedures. The US Department of Justice offers a simple plan. Following are some of highlight of plan.

A Crisis Management Plan (CNP) is a detail guideline about the policy and procedures to be followed in case of an emergency situation. The plan suggests the constitution of a Crisis Management Team (CMT) and an Evacuation Team (ET).

The goals of the CMP are the following:

- Provide guidance to managers regarding proper procedures and resources.
- Protect the safety and well-being of all employees.
- Provide for the care of employees and their families through personal services.
- Minimize post-traumatic stress reaction among employees.
- Ensure that accurate and appropriate information about the incident is conveyed to appropriate audience.
- Plan the orderly return of the work place to a normal mode of operation.
- Outline preventive measure to be taken in advance.

The Crisis Management Team is the team responsible for responding to the emergency situation and could include the following:

- **Crisis Manager**
- **Administrative Coordinator**
- **Operations Coordinator**

- **Technical Support Coordinator and**
- **Employees Support Coordinators**

All these individuals should be present during the period of operation, should have leadership quality and sound judgment under any pressure arising due to a crisis and should communicate clearly. The problem of availability during the event especially one with multiple sessions and limited number of the venue team available at the leased premises. The members of CMT must be well trained and experienced in facing the crisis situation. The following are the main roles of each individual in the CMT:

Crisis Manager

The crisis manager will have the responsibility of managing the crisis on the event venue. He will be assisted by the CMT. The duties of the Crisis Manager will be to ascertain the nature and location of the emergency sport and decide the appropriate action to insure that the Evacuation Team members are advised properly about the evacuation and brief the emergency personnel on their arrival.

Administrative Coordinator

The administrative coordinator will locate, procure and store items listed in the emergency equipment and supply a list before any crisis. He will provide administrative support needs of the CMT and work in close coordination with the Crisis Manager. He will issue notifications and mobilize resources and collect and distribute documents.

Operation Coordinator

In order to maintain operational efficiency, the Operations Coordinator will act as a liaising man between the CMT and other operations staff. He will also assess and identify the operational needs, coordinate transportation and assist in bringing the operations to normal ones.

Employee Support Coordinator

The employee support coordinator will coordinate family support and trauma recovery. He will provide psychological services to all victims, family members and co-workers.

Technical Support Coordinator

The technical support coordinator is responsible for setting up equipment for the command center and other areas. He will ensure the functioning of proper telecommunications lines and monitor the televised newscasts and proper functioning of the computers and telephone lines.

For big events, the Evacuation Team might also include the following personnel:

- **Floor Monitor.**
- **Staircase Monitors.**
- **Handicap Person Monitor.**

The floor monitor would supervise and expedite the movement of individuals in a planned and controlled way, at his assigned floor. He will remain in constant touch with the Staircase Monitor through the use of two-way radios or mobile phones. The Staircase Monitor would be responsible for controlled movement of individuals and remain in constant communication with the Floor Monitor. Handicapped person monitor will assist physically challenged persons during the evacuation process. He will report the status of the handicapped persons to the floor monitor.

Implementation of Emergency Procedures

In order to implement emergency procedures effectively the following action should be taken:

- Review implementation procedure and integrate with overall event operational plans.

- Ensure complete awareness of the procedure among all concerned, by disseminating information and wide consultations.
- Provide required information through the use of signage and designed communication materials.
- Train all staff about their role in emergency.
- Rehearsals of conducting evacuation exercises.
- Review and make necessary changes in the procedures to ensure its effectiveness.
- Study the Action Taken Report of previous events under different crises.

Fire Procedures

Normally the following steps should be taken in case of any fire at the event venue:

- Ensure the safety of every one within the vicinity of the fire.
- Call the Fire Services department in case of any suspension of fire.
- Start immediately evacuation in accordance with evacuation procedures.
- Fight the fire with the available fire extinguisher cylinders and other available equipment or retreat and close all doors

Evacuation Procedures

A crisis management plan relies on the chain of command and an early warning system for a fast intervention. During the evacuation certain personal traits and characters are required to be shown by all staff:

- Remain calm.
- Be observant.
- Listen to and follow all instructions strictly and diligently.
- Provide all information and instruction to all staff and spectators.
- Follow all safety precautions laid down for such situations.

Event Crisis Management

Companies face crisis all the time a company leader making a poor personal decision, product recalls, event planner becomes the very significant in cases like fire mishap.

Event planners must consider a crisis plan as an insurance policy for the corporate image when such a plan is in place with an examination of potential scenarios, one can spend crucial time on implementing the plan, rather than to brooding over from where to start, as and when a crisis hits. Event managers can gather as much information about the situation as quickly as possible from varied sources. The preparedness includes developing a detailed crisis strategy, creating and compiling materials for media in advance and creating a pre-crisis team. Event planner is responsible for the entire event and his responsibility somewhat more than that of the client.

While no one can predict a crisis, appropriate foresight and thinking can make a difference between maintaining a healthy corporate image and the dreadful alternative. The event planners should remain prepared with solution in advance for impending and possible problems and have action plans for any emergency.

The first step in planning in event crisis management is to understand which people or person will control in case of any emergency the crisis team should discuss possible emergency scenarios and decide, in advance, what the action plan will be and will man which point and respective roles well defined and clearly communicated.

If possible, mock drills may be conducted. The alternative person should be kept ready to replace a person who might be got injured in the emergency arisen.

Problems and hurdles could be tolerated before the start of the event, but may not be acceptable in between the event. The event industry has to face manifold problems and crises. A good event planner must have done proper planning for saving time and money to avoid any apprehended crisis and planning to keep the damages at the barest minimum level.

All stakeholders are analogous to families in personal crisis. Preparing for the crucial phases ahead of time will allow the event management agencies to minimize vulnerability and panic conceptualization of event planning to stage it in practicality, is appreciated by different cadre of professionals involved in the trade of event management. Event management expert face disastrous problems and situation, which force them to change the course and the point of action, which they have been avoiding so far.

The bottom line is that when there is a crisis, the management expects that the Chief Communicator take charge and handle it. The process in many communication plans fails to represent accurately the real world, the way in which the things get done in the organization. The users of any crisis plan want simple, step-by-step instructions which clearly tell them what they must do and when and what the responsibilities of their fellow manager will be. At times when an actual crisis does occur, the specifics of the situation may be unique and unprecedented, one of the first thing to do, will be to start from the scratch.

The expert event planner can offer an organization the expertise required for an effective communication campaign, as he possesses a vast experience of directing and managing public relations campaign. The management presupposes that the communication chief is fully prepared and geared up to confront any such situation arising.

SUGGESTED QUESTIONS

1. What is the importance of contingency plan in event management?
2. What are the key things in drawing a crowd management plan?
3. How does a crowd management and evacuation plan differ from each other depending on the venue of the event?

4. What are the major risks to be consider in relation to crowd management and evacuation plan?
5. What are the goals of a crowd management plan?
6. Who should be essentially included in the crisis management team?
7. What is the importance of crisis management plan for the corporate image?

12

MONITORING, CONTROL AND EVALUATION

Control System

Control systems are essential for ensuring that procedures are followed and that performance measures are achieved. For example, in case of cash handling in which all entries, including deposit and withdrawal of case are dully recorded in the cash book. Evaluation is the process of measuring the success of an event against its objectives.

Monitoring and Control System

A successful event manager needs to delegate the works to his subordinates and monitor the same effectively. All routine procedures and control systems need to be put in place before the event starts. Such control systems would insure the passing on all information to the top of the event organization and help the management to take a decision whether to intervene during the hours of the event. The top management, generally, would like to intervene only if the things are not going according to the plan. A simple procedure can be followed by recording the number of boxes of stock received and issued. An hourly check of stock and cash past over the counter would immediately show the shortfall if any.

The controls are mainly of two types; preventive and feed back. A preventive control is put in place early in the planning process. Signed recognition forms are preventive measures designed to check unauthorized spending. A check list for sporting equipment before the Commonwealth Games, 2010 will be another example of preventive control measure. The designed setup would meet international specifications. In case of any inaccurate measurements, it may cause injury to an athlete and may also disqualify an athlete. To check the quality of food by monitoring food temperatures to ensure healthy food could be another preventive control measure. Normally a site inspection check list may include the following:

- Suitability of food and beverage preparation and service areas.
- Capacity for storage.
- Accessibility for delivery and installation of equipment.
- Fixed and rental equipment requirements.
- Capacity for sitting and standing spectators.
- Electrical and water supply.
- Sight lines for event audience.
- Proper setting places for recording equipment and live broadcast.
- Emergency evacuation plan.
- Accessibility of emergency services like fire tenders, ambulances.

Feedback Control Systems

Feedback control systems are put in place to assist the decision makers during an event. To keep a control over the event merchandise a feedback control system would be required at the nick of time. If the stock of left over merchandise is discounted too early, the organizer lose the revenue, if the same is discounted too late, the organizer is left with the stock that has no re-sale value once the event is over. So incident reporting is another form of feedback control. If similar incidents have occurred during the previous events, preventive measures need to be implemented.

In most industries, information from the point of sale and stock control system is the feedback for measuring and managing sales and profit positions during a particular period. However, in the event industry, decisions about price and product features are made well before the event. It is also very important to collect and store information on items such as merchandise sales, and the suitability of the left over stock for use for the next event of similar nature.

Operational Procedures for Monitoring and Control Systems

There are a number of issues in relation to operational procedures that need to be addressed before the event begins. These include the necessity for delegation of responsibility and flexibility in carrying out procedures, the effect of control systems on customers, and the importance of financial controls.

Implementation of High-Risk Procedures

If the procedure is one that involves high risk, it must be fixed, detailed and documented. It must be a part of training and be readily available to those who need it. The procedure for emergency evacuation is a good example during the training on evacuation. Poster and signs must be erected to assist in remembering. Under emergency systems, controls must be put in to check fire fighting equipment, crowd management equipment and exit and access for emergency vehicles.

Delegation of Decision Making Roles

At most events, the pace of incidence is so fast that it is crucial for staff to be in positions to make decisions on the spot. For the successful operation of an event it is necessary that some parts of the event manager's role to be delegated. Volunteers are also in need to know the part to be played by them in the problem solving process. However, important matters such as evacuation are required to be referred to senior staff on duty. Event staffs need to be trained to make decisions making when incidence minor occurs and should be analyzed at the end of shift or at the end of the day. In order to ensure quality service and contain the cost, checks and monitoring should be done to ensure that delegation is functioning well.

Flexibility in Operational Procedures

Flexibility is required in many aspects of event management, particularly during the operational phase. For this, it is important that all staff must fully understand the desired outcomes. Staff also need to think and believe in themselves and make quick decisions about changing non-critical procedures, as and when circumstances demand it. This ability on the part of the staff is one of the most desirable qualities of event operations staff.

Balancing the Customer Satisfaction and Lawlessness

Some times, control systems can frustrate customers and at times, customers will endeavor to circumvent the system. The customers can try to disturb the system by adopting any of the following:

- Enter areas without accreditation.
- Change their seating to a better area.
- Cross crowd control barriers.
- Stand or sit in the aisles.

In any of such cases, a decision needs to be made by the event staff on the spot as to what to do. If a customer is refusing to wear safety gears for a ride, customer safety consideration should come before customer satisfaction. On the other hand if a customer wants to not walk an extra distance due to crowd control barriers and when there are virtually no crowds, the staff on the spot may decide to move the barriers to allow the customers go through.

Controlling Finances

For the successful conclusion of an event, it is necessary that expenditure is made according to budgeted amount through a financial control system. This system can be ensuring by the following measures:

- Using a requisition system for purchase/ expenditure to keep in limit the authorized staff to spend over a certain limits.
- Ensuring that all expenditure is accounted for and well documented.

- Checking goods against requisition slips and orders forms.
- Checking all stock and stock levels.
- Using financial systems maintaining up-to date information on income and expenditure.
- Using financial systems to forecast cash flow.
- Ensuring that every staff understands the budget and financial position.

Control of Sales Registers

Control of sale system and sale register can be achieved by the following measures:

- Checking that cash received is properly recorded and process through the point-of-sale system and sales register.
- Checking the point-of-sale register print out have been balanced against cash drawn.
- Checking the transportation and storing of all cash and document.
- Checking that all banking documentation has been retained and balanced against statement issued by the bank.

Some experienced event organizers have suggested the following for monitoring and controlling event operations:

- Check everything over and over.
- Write every thing down, including promises made by your contractors and requests made by your client.
- Develop check list for everything possible.
- Check the venue before you move in, and note any existing damage.
- Never leave the venue until the last staff member has finished.
- Check the venue before leaving; something may have been accidentally left on (gas) or left behind (including people).
- Pay attention to details at every stage.
- Schedule carefully, since the audience has little patience with long-winded speeches, for example.
- Maintain a contingency fund for unexpected expenses.
- Involve the sponsor at every stage.

- Get approvals for use of logos before printing.
- Don't take safety knowledge for granted; repeat often.
- Train staff to be observant.
- Check everything, over and over.

Evaluation

Evaluation is an area that is frequently neglected following an event. This neglect is generally for the sake of convenience. For the sake of quality control it is necessary and provides many benefits to be gained from an evaluation critically. It provides an opportunity to those involved in organizing and staging an event. The organizers can learn from the shortcomings pointed out by the experts and improve operations during events in future. It also provides a lot of information for future planners of events it can supplement your own experience from the experiences of some one else.

The event objectives are generally the guiding principles of the evaluation process. An annual research into the demographics and audience behavior of the audience has been a contributing factor to the outcome of the evaluation. This also enables the event organizers to plan for the future events and improve the figure from year to year. In addition to the planning of the event it can also help the organizers in the concept of developing event aims and objectives, understanding of the target audience and consumer's decision making processes.

Evaluation Method

For planning a proper evaluation, it is necessary to work out what information is required for an evaluation. The information about the age and address of the participants would allow an analysis in terms of their general demographics. The information about the previous participation and the basis and information of the decision of the participants would also assist the organizers of the future events.

This type of information can be obtained before, during and after an event by getting forms filled in or through personal interviews. A small focus group of participants can also provide valuable information through group discussion.

In order to obtain a more reliable report, the survey needs to be designed and analyzed by a professional market research agency. The questionnaire method is a normal method of an informal post-event process. The questions in the survey may include the following:

- How did you decide to participate in the event?
- Why did you decide to participate in event?
- When did you decide to participate in the event?
- Did you come to the event alone or with other people?
- Who was the main decision maker?
- Did this event come to your expectation?
- Did you get value for your money?
- Were the food and beverage to your liking?
- Did you find the seating, light, sound and vision convenient?
- Would you attend this event again or not?
- Would you recommend/not recommend the event to others?
- Have any suggestion for the improvement?

For the evaluation an exhibition the following questions may be included in the questionnaire:

- Why did you come to this exhibition?
- Did you place any orders in this exhibition or plan to place any?
- Did you come to this exhibition earlier also?
- What were the best features of the exhibitions in your view?
- Have you any suggestions to improve the exhibition further?

Meetings with Staff and Stakeholders

Meetings with event staff and stakeholder can provide valuable information for the evaluation report. Some of the questions raised in such meetings may include the following:

- What went well and why?
- What went badly and why?
- How could the operations be improved?
- Are there any shortcomings in the recruitments and training?
- What can we learn from this event?

Financial Statements

An audited financial record and other documents are essential components of a post-event analysis and reporting. These documents may include the following:

- Audited financial statements.
- Budget papers.
- Revenue, expenditure and bank account details.
- Sale reconciliation report.
- Pay roll records.
- Insurance policy.
- Papers and records relating to contracts and agreement with other agencies.
- Asset register.
- Event evaluation and statistics.
- Event report.
- Sponsor report.

It is an important tool to know that the event organizer has managed a successful event and also a proof of a successful management. The event manager needs more than managing the event successfully.

SUGGESTED QUESTIONS

1. What is the importance of monitoring and control system in an event management?
2. What are the functions of feed back control system for decision makers during an even?
3. How are high risk procedure implemented?
4. Why are decisions making roles delegated for an efficient monitoring and control system?
5. How could the event manager balance between customer satisfaction and lawlessness of the crowd?
6. What is the importance of evaluation in quality control in event management?

13

CAREERS IN EVENT MANAGEMENT

Booming Event Industries

The new economic policy of the Government of India provided new impetus to the event industry. In addition to traditional cultural festivals, measures to boost up the industries, added new feathers to the high flying event industry all over the world, in general and in India in particular.

Cultural festivals include art festivals, classical music festivals, film festivals, dance and craft festivals, couture festivals, social festivals like Bihu festivals of Assam, Onam of Kerala, Baisakhi of Punjab and a number of sports events. The events conducted by different industrial houses and industry associations, like FICCI, ASSOCHAL and others include meetings conferences and exhibitions organized both annually and occasionally. One of the examples is the international trade fare being organized annually by the India International Trade Fair Authority at Pragati Maidan from November 19 to November 25. Industries contribute to the total number of event in India as they do all product launches and large scale private parties.

The crowd management and the crowd control are the most problematic areas in event management. Event organizers are obliged to ensure the safety of the staff, the audience and other participants by applying latest knowledge and technology. A good knowledge of spectators' psychology can help to predict the crowd behavior and probable problems likely to occur.

An event manager needs to have a sound knowledge of human psychology, crowd behavior, consumer decision making process, financial management, and human resource management marketing of event, safety measures before, during and after the event, evacuation measures. The role of an event manager is a hard work with long hours, but it is an eventful and blossoming career and if performed professionally and diligently, it may turn out to be a fun. Once the spectators come out of the event gates, with happy and excited faces, the event manager has also a beaming face. The event industry provides an adrenalin rush for those involved in the business.

Blossoming and Eventful Career

Of late, event management profession has turned out to be a blossoming and eventful career. In addition to the post of Event Manager, there are many other jobs available in the event industry. In absence of sufficient number of person with requisite education, training and experience, people often having come from other fields, such as sport administration, entertainment, television production and with a medical background could be found working on event management. Apart from the post of event manager, the others jobs available in the event industry include the following:

- Venue Manager
- Venue Registration Manager
- Entertainment Manager
- Administration Coordinator
- Security Coordinator
- Risk Manager
- Catering and Waste Manager
- Lighting and Sound Engineer
- Exhibitions Managers
- Communication Manager
- Event Designer.

- Sponsorship Manager.
- Operations Coordinator.
- Employee Support Coordinator.
- Technical Support Coordinator.
- Floor Coordinator.
- Staircase Monitor
- Handicapped Persons Monitor.

Job Descriptions

Event Manager

The roles performed by an event manager are varied and multiple. Some duties that he has to perform that may be found in the job descriptions of an event manager, are the following:

- Develop an event concept, purpose and objectives
- Constitute a committee or an event planning team for the event
- Review the event to maximize its strength and opportunity
- Undertake a risk management analysis and conduct a mock drill to minimize the risk and prompt action
- Develop a marketing plan for the event
- Prepare budget break- even and cash flow analysis
- Obtain the approval of stakeholders for the event plan
- Organize specific theme
- Recruit and select staff, train them and lead them properly
- Prepare detailed plans for the safety and security of the event, including emergency measures like fire fighting and evacuation procedure
- Prepare procedure for event logistic and its actual operation
- Keep ready monitoring and control systems
- Prepare evaluations procedures
- Present a post-event evaluation report to sponsors and other stake holders

Venue Manager

The venue manager, who is a permanent employee of the venue of the event, is quite familiar with all aspects of the venue and provides guidance services to anyone who hires the venue for the successful organization of an event. A close coordination between the Venue Manager and the Event Manager is essential, especially on account of the fact that both belong to different organizations. Sometimes the issue of hiring a security contractor and cleaning contractor can lead to a conflict of opinion and experience of working with different service providers by the two. At times they may prefer different service providers and suppliers for the reasons non to them only.

Duties of a Venue Manager

- Develop a site diagram, site dimensions and specifications.
- Negotiate contracts and fees.
- Negotiate organizational structure and staffing with the event organizer.
- Discuss site needs for performers.
- Discuss site needs for the event audience/spectators.
- Review the plans for logistics and operations.
- Provide support for setup, including signs and crowd management facilities.
- Ensure development and implementation of safety and security plans.
- Monitor the site for health, safety and cleanliness.
- Work with the event team to ensure that the emergency evacuation plan is in place and that roles are clear.
- Check entrances, exits and equipment (i.e., public address system, security communication system).
- Assist with teardown at the end of the event.
- Check all assets and monitor security during teardown.
- Manage payment of fees.

Exhibition Registration Manager

The registration of people visiting an exhibition is a key role, and in many cases exhibition organizers do their best to register participants beforehand for two reasons: it saves time on entry to the exhibition, and it allows for the registration of participants who intend to visit but do not make it on the day. When completing the registration form, the person indicates his or her area of interest in the exhibition and this information allows exhibitors to target this person for advertising. The database of visitors to an exhibition is a most valuable asset. Therefore, technical hitches must be avoided at all cost because they can cause delay and at worst, loss of data. (One exhibition manager reported that the loss of his data resulted from a power surge to his computer.)

Duties

- Meet with the committee/organizer to establish registration requirements, in particular the system for registration and the data to be captured.
- Develop a registration plan, including selection of software or specialist subcontractor and a schedule for the complete process.
- Develop an operational plan and diagram for the registration area and review feasibility with the venue concerned, with particular emphasis on network cabling and backup electrical supply.
- Recruit, select and train staff for registration duties.
- Assist with planning of advance mail-out advertising and information on pre- registration.
- Organize name tags, magnetic cards or other materials for registrations.
- Setup organizers areas.
- Allocate duties to staff and schedule tasks to suit level of demand.
- Manage operational issues, questions, problems and complaints.
- Monitor and manage those waiting in lines.
- Close registration and provide required reports to exhibition managers.

Crisis Manager

The Crisis Manager will have the responsibility of managing the crisis on the event venue. He will be assisted by the CMT. The duties of the Crisis Manager will be to ascertain the nature and location of the emergency spot and decide the appropriate action to ensure that the Evacuation Team members are advised properly about the evacuation and brief the emergency personnel on their arrival.

Administrative Coordinator

The Administrative Coordinator will locate, procure and store items listed in the emergency equipment and supply a list before any crisis. He will provide administrative support needs of the CMT and work in close coordination with the Crisis Manager. He will issue notifications and mobilized resources and collect and distribute documents.

Operation Coordinator

In order to maintain operational efficiency, the Operation Coordinator will act as a liaising man between the CMT and other operation staff. He will also assess and identify the operational needs, coordinate transportation and assist in bringing the operations to a normal ones.

Employee Support Coordinator

The Employee Support Coordinator will coordinate family support and trauma recovery. He will provide psychological services to all victims, family members and co-workers.

Technical Support Coordinator

The Technical Support Coordinator is responsible for setting up equipment for the command center and other areas. He will ensure the functioning of proper telecommunications lines and monitor the televised newscasts and proper functioning of the computers and telephone lines.

For big events, the Evacuation Team might also include the following personal:

- **Floor Monitor.**
- **Staircase Monitors.**
- **Handicap Person Monitor.**

The Floor Monitor would supervise and expedite the movement of individuals in a planed and controlled way, at his assigned floor. He will remain in constant touch with the Staircase Monitor through the use of two-way radios or mobile phones. The Staircase Monitor would be responsible for controlled movement of individuals and remain in constant communication with the Floor Monitor. Handicapped Person Monitor will assist physically challenged persons during the evacuation process. He will report the status of the handicapped persons to the floor monitor.

The position available in the event industry are many and varied. Quite often people find themselves working on events, having come from other field such as sport administration, entertainment, television production, and even nursing. Medical background can be highly relevant to other roles such as first-aid training and occupational health and safety training, leading ultimately to a role in risk management.

Anyone planning a career in events must stay up-to-the-minutes with trends in entertainment and the arts.

BOOMING EVENT INDUSTRY

Of late, event management industry has emerged as the fastest growing industries in India. Events are now acknowledged as an image builder option leading to greater development. It is also opening brighter and prospective career opportunities for young job seekers. As India is hosting the Commonwealth Games, 2010, it going to be the biggest ever event organized in India. By any estimate, the turnover of the common wealth Games, 2010 will come around 3,000 crores. It has vast employment opportunities from infrastructure to organizing the actual event.

It means to event industry-Job opportunities in huge number and resultant shortage of skilled manpower/managers. As the event industry is growing, so the Job opportunity which is a natural consequence of any growing industry.

According to a study conducted by the Federation of Indian Chambers of Commerce and Industry (FICCI), Event Management is a multi-crore industry with mega shows and events regularly hosted in India. Even personal functions like marriage and birthday parties are being managed by professionals. The growth of mega and sophisticated companies have brought in its corollary, meetings seminars, conferences, product launch, etc in great style and professionally managed.

Events expenses which were 20 crores during 90s, grew to 500 crores by 2000. According to an estimate of the FICCI, event management industry is going to be a 3,500 crore industry by 2005 and to 10,000 crore by 2010-11.

But due to shortage of trained event managers companies are not finding their executives fully equal to the task, say, some where near international standards, to manage the events. According to a research paper there was no formalized education system or course to teach event management formally. But now a number of Institutes, both in government and private sector, have started courses in the Event Management. But still they lack facilities and infrastructure to train event managers of international standards. After all event management includes a number of qualities and skills of technical knowledge, organizational skills, public relations marketing, advertising, catering, logistics, décor, human relations, risk management and above all expertise in media handling and working of various media.

As a conglomerate of a number of professions, the event management profession is still and continue to be a complex learning situation for young students. It is basically an extension of public relations and corporate communication. It has branched off from public relations. The live entertainment industry and event management industry are virtually segments of entertainment industry. Event management involves the planning, organizing and executions of events. Creative department is an integral part of the event management from the beginning to the end, from proposal to presentation of the event. While productions handles the logistics of organizing the event, marketing shoulders the responsibility of setting the event, the creative department conceptualizes the entire concepts.

Wedding planners are high in demand all around the globe. In India, the wedding industry attached a lot of money and glamour to the wedding arrangements. Tailor made weddings are the order of the day. Wedding manager offer a package consisting of the entire arrangement for the wedding, right from the engagement to honeymoon. Even commoners in large numbers would now like to utilize the services of event planners to turn their marriage event as memorable.

For entertainment industry, event management has become indispensable and for promoting any product and attracting customers, entertainment is the buzz word today. Be it the Olympic Games, FIFA World Football Cup, the Commonwealth Games or launching of a product or fashion couture, events manager have come much into great demands.

According an expert from the industry, an event manager requires "High amount of creativity, ability to work as a team, presence of mind, flexibility in terms of working hours, tactful to handle celebrities to even to a worker, are the characteristics required out of an event manager."

Facing the shortage of trained and holding a formal professional qualifications, a number of corporate houses and institutes, have now started imparting training in the area of event management. Simultaneously, the profession provides a good scope for starting one's own firm, similarly on the lines of public relations, CA, etc.

Event planning is taken to new levels of success when strategic thinking is combined with creative process. Managerial aspects of event management combines both marketing and PR-communication skills. Clients need to know the capability and strength of the event planner. India as a market is capable of proving a big platform to conduct the business and it is in favor of budding event planners to enter into the trade which has opened enormous opportunities.

Planners and organizers must make sure that protocol, business etiquette culture and customs become parts of the event planning process.

India is a country of multi-culture and diversified culture. Different communities have their own set of preferences likes and dislikes, event planner must be aware of cultural diversity and must keep in mind what all could be used to project efficient event planning and what all should be avoided to keep the rhythm of the event working in a smooth manner.

In India we have a rich tradition of various handicrafts, handlooms and other art work produce by our artisans these represent not only our heritage and culture but also great shopping attractions. Most of the foreigners coming to India want to learn about its culture. Culture is absorbed by acquainting oneself with language, food, dress and traditional arts and culture. In many parts of India there are informal market places called haats. These are generally seen in village clusters, small towns and even state capital cities.

In rural areas festival and fares are linked with harvesting seasons and selling of grain and cattle. The exact dates of these festivals depend on the lunar calendar. These fares are appropriate destinations to get experience of something new both for the client and the event management team. Such destinations are not available in cities. The arts and crafts mela organized annually at Faridabad (Haryana), is the rare example of such a rural haat where arts and crafts not only from different states of India, but also from a number of other countries are exhibited in abundance. If your client is someone from abroad and they want to experience the Indian culture from a close angle, a trip to this place could be an incentive travel award for your clients.

Pushkar Mela

Pushkar mela is one of the largest fairs in India. It is held at Pushkar in Ajamer District of Rajasthan every year in October-November. It attracts lakhs of people not only from different parts of Rajasthan and neighboring states, but from all over India and from a number of foreign countries. The camel riding is especially very popular among foreign tourists. Tens of thousands of camel and cattle are sold during the mela. There are camel races and singing and dancing by local folk artists attired in traditional Rajasthani dresses, which are of utter astonishment and pleasure of foreign tourists. There is a brisk sale of musical instruments popular among local community, camel trappings, leather moiris, hand spun and hand woven woolen shawls and blankets. Different kinds of handicrafts, puppets, trinkets and pieces of embroidery done by women of Barmer and Jaisalmer are sold at Puskar Mela.

Puri Rath Yatra

Rath yatra of Lord Jagannath also known as car Festival at Puri is one of the largest gathering of human population moving in drove pulling a wooden cart. It is the grandest of all festival in Orissa. Every year the Rath Yatra is a sacred journey of Lord Jagannath, with brother Balabhadra and bahen (sister) Subhadra from the main Jagarnath Temple on Rath (a newly built wooden cart) to another shrine called Gundicha Mandir for nine days, pulled by thousands of devotees for days together and are taken back and put in the main Jagannath Temple, with all rituals and devotion. It is said that only once in a year, Lord Jagannath come out the temple to give Darashan to His devotees. Both sides of roads from Puri to Bhubaneshwar, that passes through villages shops are displayed with beautiful hangings. Many cooperative societies find such opportunities useful to market their handloom products particularly from Sambalpur of Orissa.

Khajuraho Festival

Khajuraho Festival is an annual event of dance and music held in the month of March in Khajuraho in Madhya Pradesh. Artist of national eminence are invited to perform. The Festival was first organized in 1975 by the Madhya Pradesh Tourism Development Corporation to coincide with the India Tourism Year. The Idea of using temples for tourism and music has been taken up very well. It is to be noted that the origin of all classical music and dances in India have been in the temples. In case of Khajuraho temples, the sculptures themselves invoke, beckon and inspire artists. The temple walls are ornamentally decorated with horizontal bands of intricately carved figures. A large number of individual figures of gods, goddess, voluptuous women, mythical best and couples in erotic postures provide an astonishing scene.

Khajuraho Festival was originally planned as a festival of local Bundelkhandi music and dance forms, to be held every year in December. The venue was the Kandariya Mahadeo temple in the western groups of temples. The festival is publicized both at local state and national level. A number of tourist brochures published by Tourism Department of the Government of Madhya Pradesh mentions Khajuraho Festival as prominent tourist attraction. This Festival is an important event, and in coming year the event management agency and corporate event planners would be using Khajuraho as a destination for organizing events. After economic liberalization, multinational corporations are increasing their stake in Indian economy, and use of destination of traditional value is also on the increase, as business has also become an integral part of societal development and corporate social responsibility (CSR).

Tourism Events of India

India being a country of diversified cultures having some of the world's oldest sculptures, is a unique destination for those who want to see the special features of diversified cultures. The event manager and event management agency which deal in organizing event at different locations have to specialize in tourism events, have to perform in a planed manner. Clients expect glimpses of native culture during their visit. Travelers have been welcomed to join and participate in festivals, rituals, ceremonies and performances. Tourism events also contribute to international understanding and harmony. The effects of tourism and the industries on society and cultures of local communities are enormous. But in fact, the socio-cultural effects of tourism can not be distinguished from those of modernization in general.

Event industry as well as tourism industry has tremendous capacity to create both direct and indirect employment opportunities. For example, the Dal Lake in Jammu and Kashmir provides direct employment to hundreds of boatmen. It also generates indirect employment to various people in and around the area. The multiplier effects of the event industry become greater when they buy goods or services from local market. The employment and effects of events are closely inter-related and follow a common source, known as eco-tourism. The impact of tourism events is manifold, like economic impact social impact and environment impact. Tourism has proved a great force in promoting understanding among different nations, as well as within national boundaries, facilitating emotional integration.

Tourism Events and Destinations in different States

Orissa

Orissa offers all glory and beauties of nature with its sea beaches, rivers lakes waterfalls, hills, forests, whiled life and tribal culture. It also possesses a great tradition of architecture, monuments dating back to the 3rd century BC. The state is dotted with 4,000 monuments and archeological sites all over the state. They include Hindu temples, mosques, churches, ancient and medieval force places and other architecture. Among the five finest temple are the Lingaraja Temple of Shiva built in the 11th century, the Mukteswara Temple, built in the

10th century, the Rajarani Temple built in the 11th century, Sun Temple at Konark, among others.

Konark completes the golden triangle of Bhubaneshar, Puri and Konark. The Temple Chariot of the Sun on the sands of the Eastern Coast is an architectural marvel of the 13th century. It is the celestial chariot of the Sun God with twelve pairs of wheels and seven horses. The legendry Temple has sculptures covering of all aspects of life, famously known as erotic art. The Konark beach gives a view of beautiful Sun rise. Ramachandi Temple is located on the confluence of the river Kushabhadra and the sea. Chilka lake is spread over 1,100 sq. km is the largest inland lake of India, dotted with islands. Sun sets and Sun rises are memorable experiences from the lake site. Similipal National Park is one of the largest tiger reserves of India, spread over 2,750 sq. km. The forest is full of hills and water falls.

But the Jagarnath Temple of 12th century, is known for annual Rath Yatra or Car Festival is most famous festival. Every year the Rath Yatra is the sacred journey of Lord Jagannath, with brother Balabhadra and bahen (sister) Subhadra from the main Jagarnath Temple on Rath (a newly built wooden cart) to another shrine called Gundicha Mandir for nine days, pulled by thousands of devotees for nine days together and are taken back and put in the main Jagannath Temple, with all rituals and devotion.

Orissa is also well known for festivals. Orissa is also known for Odissi form of folk dances which is invariably presented during all festival of Orissa. Orissa is also renowned for tribal dances. Lok Mahotsava is organized every year at Gangadhar Mandap in Sambalpur for three days to bring the folk dances and music of Orissa to lime light. Sun God is worshiped with great religious fervor and enthusiasm during Makar Mela organized at different places including Kalijai, Atri, Ghatgaon, Keonjhar, Jashipur and Jagatsinghpur. Among other important fairs being organized in different parts of Orissa are Magha Mela, Dola, Tara Tarini Mela, and Bali Yatra. Bali Yatra is organized to commemorate the glorious past of commercial voyages to

Islands of Bali, Java and Sumatra by Oriya traders on Mahanadi river bank.

Some clients would like to enjoy the special food of the place they are visiting and Oriya food is enjoyed by all who visit Orissa. Cloth is a hot selling commodity, and all visiters want to take some cloth from the place they visited in Orissa. Sambalpur sarees are one of the unique products of Orissa.

Tourist Events and Festivals of Andhra Pradesh

Andhra Pradesh is a treasure of preserved old tradition and culture. The pace of development during preceding years has given it the name of High-Tech state. The preserved heritage coupled with High-Tech development makes Andhra Pradesh a unique destination for tourist. Event planning agencies should plan an event to provide its clients an environment where the tourist can experience the old traditions and culture along with technological development.

The monolithic statue of Lord Buddha, at the Buddha-Lumbini Lake, towering 18m high-350 ton is poised in a serene majestic in the center of Hussain Sagar Lake. This gigantic replica at the Hyderabad's rock of Gibraltor is the gateway to explore the destinations of the Buddhist circuit. Anupu, located near Nagarjuna Sagar Dam is an example of architectural model with a semblance of the third century Buddha Bihara (Buddhist University). The fine amphitheatres constructed here have a seating capacity of 1,000 spectators and takes the imagination of the viewers to the ancient realms. There are several other sacred Buddhist sites of significance in Andhra Pradesh.

Tourist and Festivals of Tamil Nadu

Tamil Nadu is famous for celebrating cultural festivals all over the year, beckoning ethnic tourist and art lovers from all over the world. The dance Festival at Mammallapuram is held on an open-air stage with monolithic rock sculptures of Pallavas in the backdrop. The gold-roofed temple with pillars depicting Lord Nataraja in 108 poses is setup at Chidambaram. The poses of Lord Nataraja are from Bharatha Natyam. Carnatic music lovers from all over the world as also from different parts of India gather together in Tamil Nadu during the Chennai Music Festival organized in December-January, every year. Tourism destinations and attraction in Tamil Nadu can be categorized under pilgrimage centers, historical monuments, hill stations/resorts, wildlife, sea beaches, waterfalls and festivals. Tamil Nadu is an amazing gift of Mother Nature. It is situated on the confluence of the Bay of Bengal, the Indian Ocean and Arabian Sea. Its southern most point at Kanya Kumari simbolises the end of Indian Territory.

Tamil Nadu the land of dosa/vada/sambar, has also given the world immensely palatable Chettinad cuisine. There are a number of picturesque and beautiful hill resorts in Tamil Nadu, including those located at Ooty, Kodiakanal, Yercaud and Elagiri. Ooty and Kodiakanal have been for ages the haven for film makers and honeymooners. There are also a number of tourist destinations in Tamil Nadu at places like Hogenakkal, Courtallam. Pagoda point and Shervaroyan Temple are some other sight seeing points. Bathing in the falls of Hogenakkal is considered to be good for health.

Marina Mammallapuram and Kanya Kumari are very popular among send and sea loving tourist visiting Tamil Nadu. Marina is lined by historic buildings such as Senate House and Chepauk Palace. The design of Poompuhar is based on the sub-merged Kaviripoompattinam. Thiruchendur is revered as one of the six seats of Lord Karthikeya. Kanya Kumari has a rock on which Swami Vivekananda sat and meditated. The state is blessed with a long coastline of 900 km and has some of the most beautiful beaches in the world.

Kanya Kumari is one of the few locations in the world that offer spectacular views of both Sun rise and Sun set. Located at the confluence of the Bay of Bengal, the Indian Ocean and the Arabian Sea, Kanya Kumari is also better known for its multicolored sands. The other attractions at Kanya Kumari are Gandhi Mandapam, Vivekanand Rock, and Kanya Kumari Ammam Temple.

Tamil Nadu has more than 12 bird sanctuaries, five national parks and eight wildlife sanctuaries. The important wildlife sanctuaries are located at Mudumalai, Point Calinere and Mundanthuria. Tamil Nadu is also home to Navagraha Temples and has all the nine planets in a cluster in radius of 60 km. Other prime locations include the main groves of Pichavaram, Pulicat Lake and the palatial Chettimad houses.

Multicultural Event Planning

Every individual who intends to enter the trade of event management must be fully aware of the tourism trade. Destination management agency work as local representative of client and play an important role in creating the event vision. Destination management agencies negotiate with their local suppliers on behalf of the event planner. Local representatives are the persons who have fostered long-term working relationship with their local supplier and provide creative ideas to the event planner. Efficient event planners are always in favor of utilizing the services of these agencies which provide them detailed information about the realities at the ground level, for which the event planner might not have the time to go through.

Local Customs and Cultures

There are a number of culture and sub-culture in India. India in itself is so full of mysteries that it becomes sometimes difficult to understand and adjust in other than our native state. The varied cultures and tradition of India are a destination full of secrets for both Indians and foreign visitors. The knowledge about the destination and the culture of the country is very important for the planner. It is essential for an event planner to understand local protocol, customs, traditions and beliefs. Clients must be informed by their event planners of what to expect, what to do how to do in a given place and situation. We find different styles of living when we travel from one place to another .

The secret of creating successful events in multicultural settings lays not only fluency in the language of communication but also in collecting information related to the cultural and social matter. Event manager should be capable of implementing the communication strategy in accordance with the plan drafted by communication expert. Miscommunication may occur if planners do not speak the language of the place they intend to hold the event. While holding any event, it should be seen that the communication strategies are pursued in the planned manner. Miscommunication can occur in the culture where we work and the chances of distortion of facts increases in the culture.

Food Habits and Event

Foods and festivals are virtually inseparable from each other. But there are very few food items that are consumed by people everywhere. It is prevalent not only among the people from different parts of the world but also among people from different parts of India. Event planners need to know not only the destinations but also the guest make up. Event planners must be aware of the food habits of the local community, where event is going to take place. It is not only the food habits of the guests, but at times the religious beliefs of the guests which become the guiding factor in serving the food items. For example, Hindus would not appreciate beef in their food items, so is the case with Buddhist community. Similarly Jews and Muslims will not accept pork. Destination management agencies should advise the event planners about the local customs, dresses and behavior of the local community. India is a country of diversity where the language and food habit change from one state to another. Guests from abroad have a lot to experience from the tastes of varied food items and culture of India.

Hot Attractions

An event manager/expert must have the knowledge of hot attraction where special event could be organized or which could be marketed as a destination for meeting, conferences, incentive tours and for other special event. It is necessary for an event expert or event planner to have relevant information about the destinations within India and also within a state as well as around a particular destination. Information about these destinations is for the use of event expert. They are required to collect as much information as possible related to destinations, packages, offers from various airlines hotels, caterers along with entertainment groups. Affordable destinations can be utilized for various type of event.

Blossoming Carrier

A carrier in event management is not only lucrative, but also blossoming and challenging. There is actually a shortage of trained and qualified people required to execute the events on such an enormity.

The enormity of the ever increasing event industry is more clear from a study report. According to a study conducted by the Federation of Indian Chambers of Commerce and Industry (FICCI), there has been a 400 per cent growth in event industry since 90s. The FICCI has also estimated the investment in event industry to increase from Rs 20 crore in 90s, to Rs 500 crore in 2000, to Rs 3,500 crore 2005 and likely to increase to 10,000 crore by 2,010- 11. These figures of investments in event industry, speak itself the volume of its expansion and job opportunities in event industry. But due to shortage of Faculty for formal education for Event Management teaching, the demand is far exceeding the supply. To fill in the existing gas between the demand and supply, some big business houses have now initiated training in the event management.

Event management is one of the popular carriers in the field of communication. The perks are high and it is one of the most blossoming professions in the field. This job entails a lot of hype like the same in carriers in PR and Advertising. Those with the background of public relations, communications, hotel industry, etc have the possibilities of being more successful in the event management job. Persons with cool brain, good communication skills and extrovert quality are more acceptable and successful than otherwise.

Initially event management was limited to the areas of big and metropolitan cities, but now it is spreading its wings to medium and small towns in the interior areas located at even far-flung places of the country. The nature of the event depends on the client who hires the event management team. It may range from product launch, fashion couture to organizing conferences at national and international levels. Other event may include press-conferences, product promotions theme parties, music concerts, road-shows etc.

Even management companies have an in-house staff of 30 to 40 people. They also hire event coordinators and artist as and when required.

The event industry in India is still scattered and might face some problems in the initial stage. With increasing demands for qualified trained and specialized persons and specialist event manager, the demands for skilled persons have been increasing. But the trade of event experts is yet to cast their full impact in competition to communication experts.

Specialists, who have been in the field for the last few years, would get a big pay packet and perks. New entrants to the profession get the opportunity to secure a comfortable position in the job market and an opportunity to rise higher in the ladder sooner than their counter parts in other similar professions. Stiff competition is yet to take place in the profession. An entry ticket may smoothen the growth in the profession without much fuss.

SUGGESTED QUESTIONS

1. How has the new economy policy influenced the growth of event industries in India?
2. What are the qualities required for a successful event manager?
3. What are the jobs available in event industries, in addition to the job of event manager?
4. What are the roles performed by an event manager?
5. What are the functions of an event manager in coordinating the event?
6. How has the event industry grown in last to decades in India?
7. Why is the knowledge of culture necessary for successfully organizing an event at a particular place?
8. How is the career in event management more lucrative in comparison to other similar professions?

14

Ethics of Event Management and Role of ISES

Code of Ethics

As with all other modern profession, the presence of code of ethics, can enhance the reputation of those involved and can assist customers to feel confident in their choice of event manager, supplier.

International Special Events Society (ISES) has devised the following code of ethics:

- Promote and increase the highest level of ethics within the profession the special event industries, while maintaining the highest standard of professional conduct,
- Strive for excellence in all aspects of our profession by performing consistently at par or above accepted industries standards,
- Use only legal and ethical means in all industries negotiations and activities,
- Protect the public against fraud and unfair practices and promote all practices which bring credit to the profession,
- Maintain adequate and appropriate insurance coverage for all business activities,
- Maintain industry standard of safety and sanitation,
- Provide truthful and accurate information with respect to the performance of duties. Use a written contract stating all changes,

services, products, performance expectations and other essential information,

- Commit to increase professional growth and knowledge, to attain educational programmes and to personally contribute expertise to meetings and journals,
- Strive to cooperate with colleagues and suppliers, employee/ employers and all persons supervise, in order to provide the highest quality service at every level,
- Subscribe to the ISES Principles of Professional Conduct and Ethics, and abide by ISES Bye-laws and Policy.

ROLE OF ISES

History of ISES

The International Special Events Society (ISES) was founded in 1987 to foster in enlightened performance through education while promoting ethical conduct. ISES works to join professionals to focus on the "event as a whole" rather than its individual parts. ISES has grown to involve nearly 3,000 members active in 30 chapters throughout the world. Membership brings together professionals from a variety of special events disciplines including caterers, meeting planners, decorators, event planners, audio-visual technicians, parties and convention, educators, journalists hotel sales managers and many more disciplines. The solid pear network, ISES provides, helps special events professionals produce out standing results for clients while establishing positive working relationships with other event colleagues.

ISES Mission

The Mission of ISES is to educate, advance and promote the special events industries and network of professionals along with other related industries. The ISES declares:

To that end, we strive to ....

- Uphold the integrity of the special events professions to the general public through our "Principles of Professional Conduct and Ethics,"

- Acquire and disseminate useful business information,
- Foster a sprit of cooperation among its members and other special events professionals and,
- Cultivate high standards of business practices.

The other functions of the ISES include the following:

Professional Development and Certification

ISES membership keeps the professional on top of the industry trends through educational programmes. Affiliation with the local chapter of ISES provide education and idea exchanges. Participation in the annual Conference for Professional Development (CPD) or other ISES-sponsored classes adds to the knowledge of participating professionals. Working towards professional accreditation enhance the professional credibility to the persons involved and makes him a Certified Special Events Professional (CSEP).

Recognition

ISES honors industries excellence award through its prestigious award, the Esprit De Corps Awards. The Award fuels a sprit of competition within designated categories. The categories within the Esprit De Corps Awards recognized the best and most creative within the special event industry. The Esprit Awards gain global visibility and recognition for ISES members through general.

Strategic Alliance

ISES and Special Events Magazine have a strategic alliance which provides benefit to ISES members. ISES recognizes Special Events magazine as "the official and premier magazine of events industry in North America" and the Special Event show as "the official and premier trade shows for the this industry in North America."

Networking

Networking means building relationship with other professionals from your region and beyond. The exchange that takes place grows your business contacts, as well as your potential client base and provides you with new employment opportunities. By committing time through membership, you invest in yourself and in the industry while gaining an industry edge. Your special event is important- the last thing you would want to worry about is the integrity of your special events profession. That's why all ISES members subscribe to the ISES Principles of Professional Conduct and Ethics.

SUGGESTED QUESTIONS

1. How does the presence of a code of ethics enhance the reputation of those involved in the profession of event management?
2. What are the codes of ethics devised by ISES?
3. What is the mission of ISES?
4. How does ISES maintain strategic alliance with ISES members?

REFERENCES

Catherwood D. W and Kirk, R.L., *The Complete Guide to Special Event Management,* John Willey and Sons, New York, 1992.

Denvy D., *Organizing Special Event and Conferences,* Pineapple press, Sarsota, Florida, 1990.

Getz, D., *Event Management and Event Tourism,* Cognizant Communication Corporation, New York, 1997.

Goldblate, J.J., *Special Events: Best Practices in Modern Event Management,* John Wiley and Sons, New York, 1997.

Hall, C. Hallmark, *Tourist Events Management and Planning,* Belhaven Press, London, 1992.

International Special Events Society, *Code of Ethics,* www.Ises.com.

Judy, Allen, *The Business of Event Planning,* Wiley, 1952.

Paul, R. and Farlhuley, *Essential of Business Communication,* New Delhi, Sultan Chand and Sons.

Wagen, Lymn Van Der and Carlos, Brenda R., *Event Management: Tourism, Cultural, Business and Sporting Events,* Pearson Education Inc (Fourth Impression, 2009.

Watt. D., *Leisure and Tourism Events Management and Organization Mannual,* Longman, London, 1992.

INDEX